TAPAS

CONVERSION TABLES

teaspoons	tablespoons,	cups,	fluid ounces	milliliters
1				5
3	1	1/16	1/2	15
6	2	1/8	1	30
	4	1/4	2	60
	5 1/3	1/3	2 1/2	75
	6	3/8	3	90
	8	1/2	4	125
		2/3	5	150
		3/4	6	175
		1	8	237
		1 1/2	12	355
		2	16	473
		3	24	710
		4	32	946

150 °C	300 °F
160 °C	325 °F
180 °C	350 °F
190 °C	375 °F
200 °C	400 °F
220 °C	425 °F
230 °C	450 °F

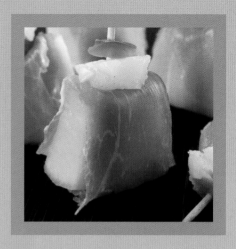

© Richard Carroll
Publisher: Richard Carroll
Project Manager: Anthony Carroll
Food Photography: David Pickett
Travel Author: Kerry Kenehan
Photography by Metz Press
Design: Lucy Adams
Editor/Proofreader: Lily Green

ISBN 13: 978 90 366 2227 1

TAPAS

TAPAS FOR EVERY OCCASION

REBO
PUBLISHERS

Walk into a Spanish tapas bar and what do you find? An exciting variety of bite-sized morsels, including tiny earthernware casseroles filled with hot dishes, tasty omelettes, little mayonnaise-topped mouthfuls and pickles on cocktail sticks. A tapas bar offers you the chance to dive into many different tastes and textures.

Although the array of food offered in a Spanish tapas bar may bewilder you at first, understand that the principle of tapas is very clear. In Spain, a tapa was to be included in the bar price of a drink – for your money you received a drink, a bite-sized taste sensation and good company. It was important that the tapa was easy to eat so it didn't interrupt the natural flow of conversation.

INTRODUCTION

The traditional drink to be enjoyed with tapas varied, but typically it was either wine, sherry or cider. You could also try wine, beer or even a celebratory sparkling wine.

Use this book to offer the same hospitality to your guests. Each recipe is accompanied by a mouth-watering photograph and clear instructions. Some of the most traditional tapas are the quickest to prepare, and you will find the tempting treats in this book simple to put together. This book will become an important part of your entertaining repetoire.

Ingredients

1 kg/2 lb chicken breasts,
  skinless, boneless

1 teaspoon ground coriander

salt and freshly ground
  black pepper

1/8 cup/1 fl oz chutney

12 slices rindless streaky
  bacon, halved

vegetable oil for
  deep-frying

toothpicks

Chicken Wrapped in Bacon

Method

1 Cut chicken breasts into strips. Mix coriander, salt, pepper and chutney and coat strips in this mixture.

2 Wrap each strip in a slice of bacon, securing it with a toothpick. Heat oil in a heavy-based saucepan, and deep-fry parcels until bacon is crisp.

3 Drain on kitchen paper and serve warm.

MAKES 24

Ingredients

¹/₂ cup/125 g cooked shrimp,
  shelled and diced

¹/₂ cup/125 g minced chicken, cooked

1 onion, finely chopped

1 tablespoon chopped parsley

¹/₂ cup/250 g mashed potato

¹/₂ cup/110 g seasoned flour

¹/₂ cup/110 g breadcrumbs

2 eggs, beaten

vegetable oil for
  deep-frying

Chicken
Croquettes

Method

1 Mix shrimp, chicken, onion, parsley and mashed potato.
If the mixture is too dry, add a drop of milk. Shape into
crescents.

2 Coat in flour, dip in beaten egg, leaving excess to drip off,
and then roll in breadcrumbs. Heat oil in a heavy-based
saucepan and deep-fry croquettes until golden
(1–2 minutes). Drain on kitchen paper and serve warm.

MAKES 12

Ingredients

500 g/1 lb chicken breasts,
   cubed

1¹/₂ tablespoons ground coriander

2 teaspoons ground turmeric

1 tablespoon ground cumin

2 teaspoons chilli powder

2 teaspoons crushed garlic

1 tablespoon brown sugar

¹/₄ cup/3 fl oz olive oil

2 teaspoons salt

16 skewers

peppers, different colors,
   cubed (optional)

Chicken
Satay

Method

1 Place chicken cubes in a bowl. Mix the rest of the ingredients and pour over chicken. Leave in the refrigerator for 4 hours, turning every hour.

2 Preheat the oven to 350 °F. Thread 3 pieces of meat onto each skewer, interspaced with peppers (if using). Place skewers on a baking tray and pour marinade over.

3 Oven-roast for 12 minutes. Remove from the baking tray and arrange on a platter with peanut sauce on the side.

MAKES 16

This is a Malay version of a shish kebab, usually marinated in a spicy paste.

Lamb, beef or pork can also be used. Add peppers for color.

Ingredients

500 g/1 lb boneless chicken breasts

1 teaspoon crushed garlic

salt and freshly ground

  black pepper

1/2 cup/5 fl oz lemon juice

1 1/2 tablespoons olive oil

1 teaspoon basil

1 teaspoon paprika

1 1/2 tablespoons honey

1 fresh pineapple, cubed

12 small sundried tomatoes

24 cocktail sticks

24 fresh basil leaves

Sweet and Sour
Chicken Kebabs

Method

1 Preheat the oven to 350 °F. Cut chicken into bite-sized pieces and place in a large bowl. Mix garlic, salt, pepper, lemon juice, olive oil, basil, paprika and honey, and pour over chicken, making sure that chicken is well covered. Leave to stand for 1 hour. Remove chicken pieces from marinade and roast in an oven pan until golden brown – about 10 minutes. Remove from the oven and allow to cool.

2 Thread chicken onto cocktail sticks with cubes of pineapple and sundried tomatoes. Garnish with fresh basil leaves.

MAKES 24

Make sure you prepare lots of these delightful bites

so that each guest can have several.

Ingredients

1 tablespoon butter

500 g/1 lb chicken livers

125 g/4^{1}/$_2$ oz bacon, diced

1 onion, chopped

1 teaspoon Worcestershire sauce

1 teaspoon tarragon vinegar

^{1}/$_2$ cup/5 fl oz brandy
   (optional)

clarified butter (optional)

salt and freshly ground
   black pepper

Chicken
Liver Pâté

Method

1 Melt butter in a large saucepan and sauté chicken livers, bacon and onion. Cook over a low heat until soft and tender. Add salt, pepper, Worcestershire sauce, tarragon vinegar and brandy (if using).

2 Bring to a boil. Place in a food processor and blend until smooth. Spoon into a serving bowl and top with clarified butter. Refrigerate overnight.

MAKES 500 mL

To make clarified butter, melt butter over low heat in a small saucepan.

Allow butter to foam without browning. Keep saucepan on low heat until

foaming stops. Remove from heat and allow to cool. Milky deposits

will settle at the bottom. Carefully pour off clear yellow liquid –

this is clarified butter.

Ingredients

200 g/7 oz beef fillet strips

3/4 cup/140 g seasoned flour

2 eggs, beaten

salt and freshly ground black pepper

1/4 cup each sesame seeds

  and breadcrumbs

oil for deep-frying

toothpicks for serving

Sesame
Beef Strips

Method

1 Coat beef strips with flour. Dip in beaten egg and toss into sesame seed and breadcrumb mix.

2 Refrigerate for about 30 minutes to allow sesame seed and breadcrumb mix to set. Heat oil in a heavy-based saucepan and deep-fry beef strips, taking great care not to overcook as this will spoil the meat.

3 Drain on kitchen paper and serve immediately with mustard.

MAKES 16 BEEF STRIPS

Ingredients

500 g/1 lb lean ground beef

1 onion, chopped

2 thick slices bread, soaked in
   1/2 cup/5 fl oz water

1 tablespoon chutney

1 teaspoon Worcestershire sauce

1 tablespoon tomato sauce

18 cheese cubes (optional)

18 toothpicks (optional)

salt and freshly ground
   black pepper

Tasty Meatballs

Method

1 Preheat the oven to 350 °F. Place meat and onion in a large bowl and mix. Mash bread and drain excess water.

2 Add bread to mince together with the rest of the ingredients, and mix well. Shape into balls, place in a casserole dish and bake for 20 minutes.

3 Drain on kitchen paper and serve on toothpicks. Serve warm, or allow to cool and serve with cheese cubes on toothpicks.

MAKES 18 SMALL MEATBALLS

Ingredients

1 egg

200 g/7 oz lean ground beef

1/4 cup/2 oz chopped onion

1 teaspoon crushed garlic

salt and freshly ground

    black pepper

1 teaspoon chutney

1 teaspoon tomato sauce

1/4 cup/2 fl oz flour

vegetable oil for frying

12 mini-hamburger rolls,

    halved and buttered

gherkins, lettuce, cocktail

    tomatoes and mustard

Mini Hamburgers

Method

1 Mix all the ingredients up to and including tomato sauce. Shape into small patties and coat with flour.

2 Heat oil in a heavy-based saucepan and fry patties. Drain on kitchen paper. Place a patty on the bottom half of each roll.

3 Top with sliced gherkin, shredded lettuce, tomato halves and a dollop of mustard. Carefully replace the top half of each roll.

MAKES 12 HAMBURGERS

Make small bread rolls, buy them ready-made,

or use a cookie cutter to cut small rolls from big hamburger rolls –

you should get 3 mini-rolls from a big hamburger roll.

Ingredients

baby carrots

button mushrooms

snow peas and young
green beans, topped
and tailed

baby sweetcorn, sweet
peppers, baby carrots,
zucchini and celery,
cut in strips

radishes, halved

pickled onions, speared
with toothpicks

cherry tomatoes

cauliflower, broken into florets

Vegetable
Crudités

Method

1 Wash vegetables thoroughly and dry on a clean kitchen
towel before arranging them on a platter.

Serve with at least 2 dips.

Enjoy fresh, raw vegetables cut or sliced in bite-sized pieces,

served with a variety of dips. They are almost essential at

any party. Make a selection of vegetables from the ingredients

list and add marinated olives for interest.

Ingredients

1 eggplant, sliced

1 large head fennel, sliced

1 yellow, red and green

   pepper, sliced

2 baby carrots, sliced

5 spring onions, sliced

5 black mushrooms

1/4 cup/2 fl oz extra

   virgin olive oil

2 teaspoons crushed garlic

2–3 ciabattas, cut into thick

   slices and lightly toasted

20 black olives

salt and freshly ground

   black pepper

Mediterranean Vegetables

Method

1 Lay the eggplant slices on a plate and sprinkle with salt. Leave for 30 minutes, rinse and pat dry. Spread all vegetables on a large baking tray and drizzle with olive oil and crushed garlic. Grill for 6 minutes, turning vegetables half-way.

2 Drizzle ciabatta slices with olive oil, pile vegetables on top, drizzle with more olive oil, and sprinkle with sea salt and freshly ground black pepper. Top with black olives and serve warm.

MAKES 20

Ingredients

1 cup/250 g self-rising flour

2 teaspoons curry powder

2 teaspoons sugar

2 eggs, separated

2 cups/1 pint milk

200 g/7 oz blanched broccoli

200 g/7 oz Cheddar, cubed

200 g/7 oz blanched cauliflower

24 wooden skewers

1/2 cup/100 g flour

vegetable oil
  for deep-frying

salt and freshly ground
  black pepper

DRESSING

1 cup/8 fl oz Bulgarian yogurt

1 tablespoon chopped fresh herbs

1/4 cup/2 fl oz tomato chutney

Deep-fried
Vegetable Kebabs

Method

1 Sift self-rising flour, curry powder and sugar into a large bowl. Make a well in the center and add egg yolk and milk. Mix until smooth. Whip egg white with a pinch of salt until it forms soft peaks and fold into the batter. Season with black pepper to taste.

MAKES 24

2 Thread a broccoli floret, a cube of cheese and a cauliflower floret onto each skewer. Toss in flour, then coat in batter. Heat oil in a heavy-based saucepan and deep-fry kebabs until golden. Drain on kitchen paper and serve with Bulgarian Yogurt Dressing. To make dressing, mix yogurt, herbs and chutney.

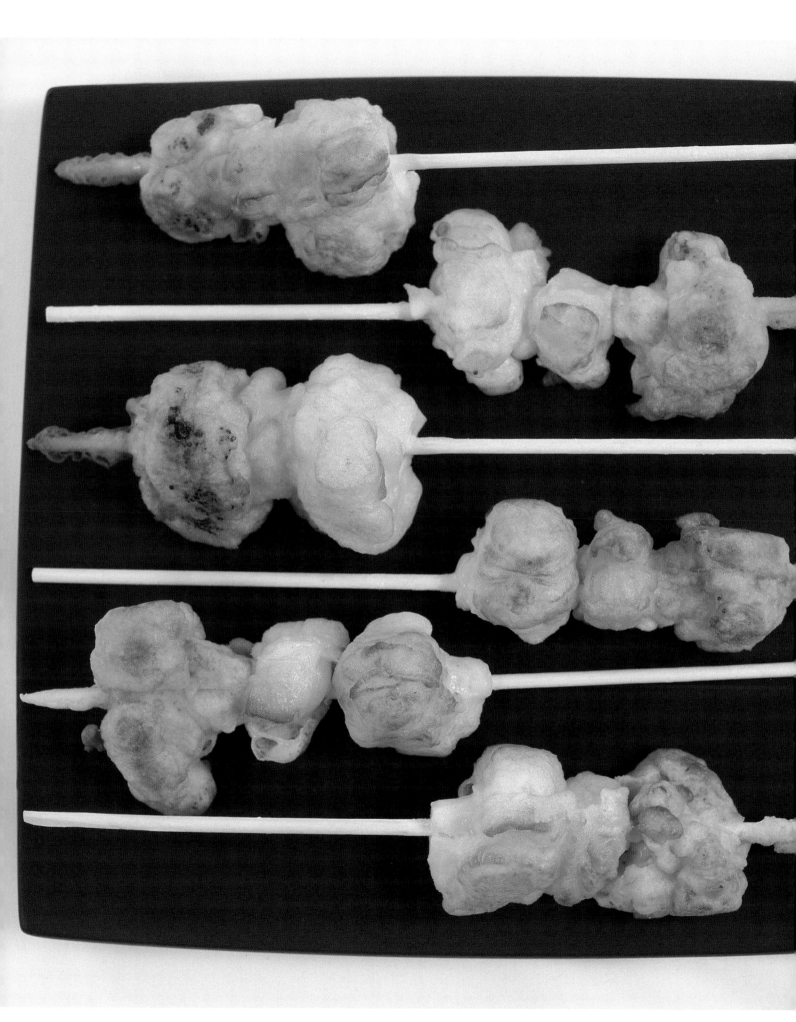

Ingredients

500 g/1 lb filo pastry

1 tablespoon melted butter

1 tablespoon olive oil

1 red pepper

1 green pepper

1 cucumber

12 cherry tomatoes

shredded lettuce

100 g/4 oz olives, pitted

3 spring onions, chopped

1 tablespoon chopped basil

6 eggs

1 tablespoon chopped

  parsley

2 tablespoons olive oil

salt and freshly ground

  black pepper

DRESSING

1 teaspoon crushed garlic

2 teaspoons mustard powder

1/4 cup/2 fl oz olive oil

2 tablespoons grape vinegar

freshly ground black pepper

2 tablespoons chopped chives

Omelette
Salad in Filo

Method

1 Preheat the oven to 350 °F. Unroll filo pastry and
keep it covered with a damp cloth.
Cut a sheet of pastry into 8 x 8 cm/4 x 4 in squares.
Brush a square with melted butter, place another square
on top of it to form a star shape and brush with melted
butter. Press into a well-greased muffin tin with pointed
ends standing up to form a basket shape (see
photograph on opposite page). Repeat with remaining
pastry. Bake for 10 minutes or until golden brown.

MAKES 12

2 Heat 1 tablespoon of olive oil in a saucepan, and fry
red and green peppers, cut into julienne strips, for
1 minute. Drain on kitchen paper and set aside to cool.
Quarter and slice cucumber and quarter tomatoes.
Combine cucumber, tomatoes, lettuce, olives, spring
onion, basil and peppers.

3 Beat eggs, add parsley, and add salt and pepper to
taste. Cook 2 omelettes over medium heat, using
2 tablespoons olive oil and a crêpe pan. Turn omelettes
out onto plate, allow to cool and cut into strips. Add to
salad vegetables.

4 To make dressing, mix all ingredients together.
Spoon omelette and salad into phyllo baskets and
sprinkle with dressing just before serving

For a non-vegetarian treat, add cubed crisp bacon, salmon strips,

or anchovy fillets to the salad before filling the filo baskets.

Ingredients

750 g/1 1/2 lb carrots, chopped

500 g/1 lb potatoes,
   peeled and chopped

1/2 teaspoon salt

3 garlic cloves, chopped

4 teaspoons cumin seeds

1 chilli, chopped

2 tablespoons lemon juice

3 tablespoons olive oil

Carrot
and Potato Dip

Method

1 Boil carrots, potatoes and salt in water until vegetables are soft. Drain and blend in a food processor with garlic, cumin, chilli and lemon juice. Gradually add oil and blend to a smooth, thick consistency.

Serve this spicy dip with fresh crusty bread or pita bread.

It is a hearty starter to a barbecue meal. It will keep your guests

happy until the first barbecued treat is ready.

Ingredients

250 g/9 oz puff pastry,
   thawed if frozen

250 g/9 oz blue cheese
   (Danish blue or stilton)

1 egg, beaten

Blue
Cheese Puffs

Method

1 Roll out pastry on a lightly floured board to a rectangle about 12 x 10 in/30 x 25 cm. Cut in half lengthways, so you have two pieces of pastry 12 x 5 in/30 x 12.5 cm.

2 Cut cheese into 16 thin fingers, about 2 in/5 cm long. Lay 2 rows of cheese, consisting of eight fingers, along the length of pastry, leaving an equal space between each. Brush around each finger of cheese with a little water. Lay the second sheet of pastry over the top and press down well between each finger of cheese.

3 Cut between cheese to make fingers about 1 1/2 in/4 cm. wide and 2 1/2 in/6 cm long. Place on a baking tray and brush with beaten egg. Chill.

4 Bake in a preheated hot oven 400°F for 15 to 20 minutes or until golden brown and puffed. Serve hot.

MAKES 16

This recipe is especially useful for the party season. You can prepare the

puffs in advance and store them on baking trays in the refrigerator. Then, as

guests arrive, it's just a matter of popping a tray into a hot oven to cook.

Ingredients

2 cups/16 fl oz natural yoghurt

1 cup/8 fl oz single cream

Yogurt
Cream Cheese

Method

1 In a bowl combine yogurt and cream. Pour mixture into a sieve lined with a double thickness of dampened muslin and set it over a bowl. Let the mixture drain for 8 hours or until the whey has drained off and the curds are firm.

MAKES ABOUT 375 ML/12 FL OZ

Ways to use Yogurt Cream Cheese

• Halve a small ripe melon, remove seeds, fill with a few spoonfuls of Yogurt Cream Cheese and sprinkle with a little soft brown sugar.

• Curl a few slices of Parma ham and serve as a first course with Yogurt Cream Cheese to which fresh herbs have been added.

• Cut the tops off 6 small tomatoes, scoop out the centers, and fill with Yogurt Cream Cheese.

• Mound about $1/2$ cup Yogurt Cream Cheese on a dessert plate, mask with sweetened very lightly whipped cream, and surround with any fresh summer fruit, or sliced and halved stewed or canned apricots, plums or peaches.

• Offer a little black pumpernickel or Scottish oatcakes with Yogurt Cream Cheese in place of a cheese board at the end of a meal.

Ingredients

1 head celery, chopped

6 tomatoes, skinned
and chopped

1 chilli, chopped

250 g/9 oz sugar

1 tablespoon salt

1 teaspoon mustard seeds

1 teaspoon allspice berries,
crushed

3 cloves, ground

1 cup/8 fl oz vinegar

Celery
and Tomato Chutney

Method

1 Combine all ingredients in a saucepan, bring to a
boil, and simmer for about 1 hour or until thick.
Ladle into sterilized jars, seal and label.

Serve with Belgian endive and ham, or with vegetable crudités.

Ingredients

1 tablespoon oil

4 dozen mussels, cleaned

60 g/2½ oz butter

¼ teaspoon garlic salt
  (optional)

Baked
Mussels in Butter

Method

1 Rub a large baking dish with oil and arrange
mussels in a single layer. Put in a very hot oven
(450°F) for 5–10 minutes, until the shells open.
Do not overcook. Remove upper shells.

2 Melt butter and add garlic salt. Serve the mussels on
the lower shells with a little butter and any liquid
that has escaped into the baking dish poured over.

SERVES 4 - 6

Ingredients

2 teaspoons salt

2¹/₄ l /4 pints natural yogurt

finely chopped mint

finely chopped marjoram

finely chopped tarragon

paprika

olive oil

Yogurt Cheese Balls
in Olive Oil and Herbs

Method

1 Line a colander or 2 large sieves with scalded muslin or cheesecloth and place over receptacle bowls to catch drainage. Whisk salt into yogurt and pour into the colander or sieves. Leave to drain overnight; it will become a soft, creamy curd. Mold this into small rounds, place them on a perforated dish and leave them in the refrigerator for 24 hours.

MAKES 16–20

2 The cheeses can be eaten straight away, sprinkled with chopped herbs or paprika and served on slices of tomato with your own home-marinated olives. If you want to keep them, leave them in the refrigerator for another 2–4 days, depending on how creamy you want them to be, then pack them into jars and cover with olive oil. Store in a cool place.

This wonderful recipe makes 16–20 small cheeses that can

be eaten straight away or stored for several months.

Ingredients

8 chicken drumsticks

2 tablespoons wholegrain
  mustard

185 g/6 oz dry breadcrumbs

1 teaspoon salt

1 teaspoon pepper

6 tablespoons/3 oz butter

2/3 cup/90 g flour

2 eggs, beaten

LIME AND MUSTARD BUTTER

9 tablespoons/5 oz butter

1 tablespoon dijon mustard

a squeeze lime juice

1/4 teaspoon cayenne

Chicken
with Mustard

Method

1 Make lime and mustard butter a few hours ahead of cooking time. Cream butter until soft, then gradually beat in dijon mustard, lime juice and cayenne. Roll it into a log shape and wrap in greaseproof paper. Refrigerate until needed.

2 Remove the skin from chicken. Mix wholegrain mustard, breadcrumbs, salt and pepper. Melt butter in a saucepan and add breadcrumb mixture. Stir until all breadcrumbs are coated with butter. Remove from the heat and leave to cool.

3 Put flour into a bowl. Beat eggs in another bowl. Take each drumstick and first coat with flour, then dip into beaten egg, and lastly press breadcrumbs over chicken.

4 Put drumsticks on a greased baking tray and bake in a preheated oven at 400°F for 45 minutes. Alternatively, cook on a barbecue. Cut lime and mustard butter into slices and serve with the chicken.

SERVES 4

This is a delicious way to eat chicken with the crisp crunchy

texture of breadcrumbs.

Ingredients

150 g/5 oz chickpeas
   (garbanzo beans), soaked

1 teaspoon salt

2 tablespoons olive oil

4 tablespoons tahina

1 teaspoon cumin seeds

juice of 2 lemons

4 garlic cloves, crushed

1 teaspoon paprika

parsley sprigs, to garnish

Hummus

Method

1 Cook chickpeas (garbanzo beans) in fresh water for about 1¼ hours or until tender. Drain. Put all ingredients except paprika and parsley into a food processor. Blend to a creamy paste. Serve on a plate dusted with paprika and garnished with parsley.

SERVES 4–6

Serve this delicious dip with pita bread, mangetout,

cherry tomatoes – anything you like.

Ingredients

500 g/1 lb radishes

1 orange

1 tablespoon unsalted butter

1/8 teaspoon salt

pepper

Radishes
with Orange Glaze

Method

1 Trim radishes of their stem and root ends and wash well. Place radishes in a steamer, cover and cook for about 15 minutes. Steaming rather than boiling is the best cooking process to use here. Radishes should be tender but still slightly firm.

2 Meanwhile, pare thin strips of rind from orange and chop it very finely, to make 1 tablespoon. Squeeze juice from orange and set it aside.

3 In a large frying pan, melt butter over a medium heat and add orange juice. Simmer for 3 minutes until the mixture becomes syrupy in texture. Transfer radishes to the frying pan, season with salt and pepper and sauté until evenly coated with orange glaze, about 2 minutes. Stir in orange rind and serve immediately.

SERVES 6

Ingredients

16 thin prosciutto slices

16 pieces rockmelon

16 pieces creamy blue cheese

16 pitted prunes

toothpicks

Air–Dried
Prosciutto Roll Ups

Method

1 Cut prosciutto slices in half lengthways.

2 Neatly roll rockmelon with prosciutto and skewer with toothpicks.

3 Roll soft blue cheese and prunes with prosciutto and skewer with toothpicks.

SERVES 8

Ingredients

500g/1 lb low-fat
   cheese, grated

ground paprika

fresh chives, chopped

fresh parsley, chopped

seasoned pepper

1 red pepper,
   finely chopped

bacon, onion and ham,
   all finely chopped
      (optional)

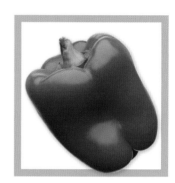

All-Purpose
Cheese Topping

Method

1 Mix all ingredients together and freeze in a small snaplock resealable bag or refrigerate until ready to use.

2 Use All-Purpose Cheese Topping as a topping for Deli Hashbrowns or mix a little of the cheese topping through scrambled eggs. Alternatively stuff mushroom caps with topping and cook in the microwave until the cheese melts. It can also be used as a pizza topping, grilled on muffins, toast or as a filling for an omelette. You could place a little on top of cooked rissoles or chicken or veal schnitzel.

SERVES 8

Ingredients

4 boneless chicken breast
    fillets, cut into 3/4-in-
    wide strips

CAJUN SPICE MIX

5 cloves garlic, crushed

4 tablespoons paprika

2 tablespoons dried oregano

2 tablespoons dried thyme

2 teaspoons salt

2 teaspoons freshly ground
    black pepper

LIME DIPPING SAUCE

1 1/2 cups/10 oz low-fat
    natural yogurt

2 tablespoons fresh lime juice

1 tablespoon finely grated
    lime rind

1 teaspoon lime juice cordial

Cajun Chicken
with Lime Sauce

Method

1 Preheat the barbecue to a high heat.

2 To make Cajun spice mix, mix garlic, paprika, oregano, thyme, salt and black pepper in a bowl to combine. Add chicken and toss to coat. Shake off excess spice mix and cook, turning frequently, on a lightly oiled barbecue plate (griddle) for 5–7 minutes or until chicken is tender.

SERVES 6

3 To make lime dipping sauce, place yogurt, lime juice, lime rind and cordial in a bowl and mix to combine. Serve with chicken.

For an attractive presentation, place a bowl of dipping sauce in the center

of a serving platter, surround with chicken and garnish with lime wedges.

Ingredients

6 rashers bacon, finely chopped

6 spring onions,
   finely chopped

4 jalapeño chillies,
   finely chopped

200 g/6¹/₂ oz packet corn chips

125 g/4 oz grated cheese
   (mature cheddar)

1 cup/8 oz sour cream

extra chopped spring onions
   to garnish

Cheese
and Bacon Nachos

Method

1 Cook bacon, spring onions and chillies in a nonstick frying pan over a medium heat for 4–5 minutes or until bacon is crisp. Remove from the frying pan and drain on absorbent kitchen paper.

2 Place corn chips in a shallow oven-proof dish and sprinkle with bacon mixture and cheese. Bake for 5-8 minutes in an oven preheated to 350°F or until heated through and cheese is melted. Serve immediately, accompanied with sour cream garnished with extra spring onions for dipping.

SERVES 6

Jalapeño chillies are the medium-to-dark green chillies that taper

to a blunt end and are 2–3 in long and $3/4$–1 in wide.

They are medium to hot in taste and are also available canned or bottled.

Ingredients

375 g/12 oz prepared puff pastry

CURRIED SAUSAGE FILLING

375 g/12 oz sausage minced

1 small carrot, finely grated

2 spring onions, chopped

1 tablespoon fruit chutney

1 teaspoon curry powder

freshly ground black pepper

Curried
Sausage Puffs

Method

1 To make filling, place sausage, carrot, spring onions, chutney, curry powder and black pepper to taste in a bowl and mix to combine. Cover and refrigerate until required.

2 Roll out pastry to 3 mm/1/8 in thick and cut out a 30 cm/12 in square. Cut pastry square in half. Divide filling into two equal portions, then shape each into

a thin sausage about 30 cm/12 in long. Place a sausage on the long edge of each pastry rectangle and roll up. Brush edges with water to seal.

3 Cut each roll into 1 cm/1/2 in thick slices, place on greased baking trays and bake for 12–15 minutes or until filling is cooked and pastry is golden and puffed.

MAKES 48

These savory puffs can be prepared to the baking stage earlier in the day.

Cover with plastic wrap and store in the refrigerator until required,

then bake as directed in the recipe.

Ingredients

8 roma tomatoes, finely chopped

1 medium red onion,
  finely chopped

10 leaves fresh basil, chopped

garlic salt to taste

1 tablespoon olive oil

2 tablespoons/1 fl oz balsamic
dressing

crusty bread loaf

a little butter

garlic salt

Fresh
Salsa

Method

1 In a bowl combine tomatoes, onion, basil, garlic salt, olive oil and balsamic vinegar.

2 Spread sliced crusty bread with butter and garlic salt. Grill or bake until golden brown.

3 Serve the fresh salsa on the hot garlic bread. This salsa is even better if prepared a few hours in advance.

SERVES 8

Ingredients

4 lean butterfly pork steaks

2 cups/16 fl oz beef stock

4 stalks celery, chopped

2 onions, chopped

FRUIT FILLING

60 g/2 oz pine nuts

100 g/3 $^1/_2$ oz pitted prunes

60 g/2 oz dried apricots

1 tablespoon grated fresh ginger

1 teaspoon chopped fresh sage

3 tablespoons fruit chutney

4 slices bacon, chopped

3 tablespoons brandy

freshly ground black pepper

Fruity
Pork Roulade

Method

1 To make fruit filling, place pine nuts, prunes, apricots, ginger, sage, chutney, bacon, brandy and black pepper to taste in a food processor and process until finely chopped.

2 Open out steaks and pound to about 5 mm/$^1/_4$ in thick. Spread filling over steaks and roll up tightly. Secure each roll with string.

SERVES 6

3 Place stock, celery and onions in a large saucepan and bring to a boil. Add pork rolls, cover and simmer for 20 minutes or until pork is cooked. Transfer pork rolls to a plate, set aside to cool, then cover and refrigerate for 2–3 hours. To serve, cut each roll into slices.

Ingredients

6 corn tortillas

CHILLI BUTTER

5¹/₂ tablespoons butter

2 teaspoons finely grated
   lemon rind

2 teaspoons sweet chilli sauce

1 teaspoon ground cumin

GUACAMOLE

1 avocado, halved,
   stoned and peeled

1 tomato, peeled and
   finely chopped

2 tablespoons lemon juice

1 tablespoon finely chopped
   fresh cilantro or parsley

Guacamole
with Tortillas

Method

1 To make chilli butter, place butter, lemon rind, chilli sauce and cumin in a bowl and mix to combine.

2 To make guacamole, place avocado in a bowl and mash with a fork. Stir in tomato, lemon juice and cilantro or parsley.

SERVES 6

3 Place tortillas in a single layer on a baking tray and heat on the barbecue for 3–5 minutes or until warm.

4 To serve, place chilli butter, guacamole and tortillas on a platter so that each person can spread a tortilla with chilli butter, top with guacamole, then roll up and eat.

Ingredients

²/₃ cup butter, softened

1 onion, chopped

2 cloves garlic, chopped

2 tablespoons fresh thyme leaves

1 tablespoon fresh rosemary leaves

750 g/1¹/₂ lb fresh chicken livers, cleaned
   and trimmed, coarsely chopped

salt

freshly ground black pepper

75 g/2¹/₂ oz rice crackers

125 g/4 oz stuffed green olives, sliced

Herb and
Liver Paté

Method

1 Melt one-third of the butter in a frying pan over
low heat, add onion, garlic, thyme and rosemary and
cook, stirring, for 6–8 minutes or until onion is very
tender.

2 Add livers to pan, increase the heat to medium and
cook, stirring, until livers are brown on the outside,
but still pink in the center. Set aside to cool.

MAKES ABOUT 30

3 Place liver mixture in a food processor, add
remaining butter, a pinch of salt and black pepper to
taste and process until smooth. Spoon mixture into a
piping bag fitted with a large star nozzle, and pipe
rosettes onto rice crackers. Arrange on a serving plate,
garnish with olive slices and serve immediately.

Ingredients

500g/1 lb pork leg steak or
  cutlet, or scotch steak

sweet chilli sauce

approximately 16 skewers,
  cut in half

MARINADE

3 garlic cloves, crushed

2 tablespoons fresh lemon grass,
chopped

1/4 cup cilantro, chopped

1 tablespoon brown sugar

1/2 teaspoon ground coriander

1/4 teaspoon white pepper

2 tablespoons salt reduced
  soy sauce

2 tablespoons fish sauce

2 tablespoons sesame oil

1/4 cup cold water

Lemon Grass
Pork Skewers

Method

1 Mix marinade ingredients together.

2 Cut pork into thin strips, thread 1 or 2 strips onto each skewer and marinate for 20 minutes or longer.

MAKES ABOUT 32

3 Heat a non-stick frying pan, barbecue plate or grill over a medium-hot heat.

4 Add oil and pan-fry pork skewers for about 1–2 minutes each side or until medium done. Avoid overcooking.

Serve these delicious pork skewers with sweet chilli sauce.

Ingredients

750 g/1½ lb lean ground beef

1 teaspoon freshly chopped ginger

1 bunch fresh chives, chopped

½ bunch fresh cilantro, chopped

1 egg

garlic steak seasoning

breadcrumbs

Low–Fat
Mini Meatballs

Method

1 Mix all the ingredients except breadcrumbs in a bowl.

2 Using a teaspoon, form small balls. Coat the meatballs with dry breadcrumbs.

3 Dry-fry the meatballs in a preheated electric frying pan lined with baking paper. (Crumbed meatballs are to be placed on top of the paper). Cook on high for 8–10 minutes, turning every couple of minutes.

SERVES 6

Next time you're having a party, cook some mini meatballs and serve

each on a toothpick. Serve with a sweet chilli sauce, fresh

chopped cilantro and a squeeze of lemon or lime juice, or wholegrain

mustard. Or you could serve meatballs on a bed of iceberg lettuce

with a bowl of tomato, barbecue sauce or any mustard sauce.

Ingredients

1 large eggplant

1 onion, unpeeled

2 cloves garlic, crushed

olive oil

2 tablespoons lemon juice

2 tablespoons chopped fresh parsley

$^{1}/_{4}$ cup/2 oz sour cream

4 pieces lavash bread,
   cut into triangles

Middle
Eastern Dip

Method

1 Preheat the barbecue to a high heat. Place eggplant and onion on the lightly oiled barbecue grill and cook, turning occasionally, for 20–30 minutes or until skins of eggplant and onion are charred and flesh is soft. Cool slightly, peel and chop roughly.

2 Place eggplant, onion, garlic, $^{1}/_{4}$ cup/2 fl oz oil and lemon juice in a food processor or blender and process until smooth. Add parsley and sour cream and mix to combine.

3 Brush bread lightly with oil and cook on the barbecue for 1–2 minutes each side or until crisp. Serve immediately with the dip.

SERVES 6

Lavash bread is a yeast-free Middle Eastern bread available from

Middle Eastern food shops and some supermarkets.

If unavailable, use pita bread instead.

Ingredients

250 g/8 oz fresh asparagus

   spears, trimmed

4 slices prosciutto or lean ham

Asparagus
wrapped in
Proscuitto

Method

1 Boil, steam or microwave asparagus until just tender. Drain and rinse under cold running water until cool. Drain asparagus again and dry on absorbent kitchen paper.

2 Cut each slice of prosciutto or ham lengthwise into 3 long strips, and wrap each strip around an asparagus spear. Cover and refrigerate until required.

MAKES ABOUT 12

Ingredients

1 bunch/90 g/3 oz watercress

1 teaspoon finely chopped
   fresh parsley

2 eggs, separated

2 tablespoons flour

freshly ground black pepper

SMOKED SALMON FILLING

60 g/2 oz cream cheese

2 tablespoons sour cream

90 g/3 oz smoked salmon

1 teaspoon lemon juice

1$^1/_2$ teaspoons gelatine
   dissolved in 1$^1/_2$ tablespoons
   hot water, cooled

Smoked Salmon
and Watercress Roulade

Method

1 Place watercress leaves, parsley, egg yolks, flour and pepper to taste in a food processor and process until mixture is smooth. Transfer watercress mixture to a bowl. Place egg whites in a bowl and beat until stiff peaks form. Fold egg white mixture into watercress mixture.

2 Spoon roulade mixture into a greased and lined 10$^1/_2$ x 12$^3/_4$ in. Swiss roll tin and bake at 350°F for 5 minutes or until just cooked. Turn roulade onto a damp kitchen towel and roll up from short side. Set aside to cool.

SERVES 10

3 To make filling, place cream cheese, sour cream, smoked salmon and lemon juice in a food processor and process until mixture is smooth. Stir gelatine mixture into smoked salmon mixture.

4 Unroll cold roulade, spread with filling and reroll. Cover and chill. Cut into slices to serve.

Ingredients

4 whole calamari

4 lettuce leaves

4 sheets nori

toothpicks

1/2 cup/4 fl oz light
    soy sauce

1/2 cup/4 fl oz water

2 tablespoons sugar

Stuffed
Calamari Rings

Method

1 Pull tentacles away from head of calamari, trim. Remove membrane from tentacles and hood and wash well.

2 Pour boiling water over lettuce leaves, and drain. Wrap tentacles in lettuce leaves, then in nori sheets, and seal with water.

MAKES 36

3 Insert tentacle parcels into calamari hoods, and secure with a toothpick.

4 Combine soy sauce, water and sugar in a saucepan, and heat gently. Add calamari parcels, cover and simmer for about 20 minutes or until tender. Remove, drain and refrigerate until cold. Serve sliced.

Ingredients

2 avocados, mashed

1/4 cup/2 fl oz
  Bulgarian yogurt

2 tablespoons olive oil

2 teaspoons crushed garlic

salt and freshly ground
  black pepper

1/4 cup finely grated onion

2 tablespoons lemon juice

Avocado
Yogurt Dip

Method

1 Neatly halve avocado and carefully scoop out the flesh before mashing. Dab the inside of each avocado half with lemon juice, then use the skins as a serving dish.

MAKES 2 CUPS/500 ML

2 Blend all the ingredients except the lemon juice with a fork or in a blender until smooth. Spoon dip into prepared avocado skins and serve.

Ingredients

1 cup/10 fl oz
  mayonnaise

1/2 cup/4 fl oz finely
  chopped onion

1/2 cup/4 fl oz chopped
  gherkins

1/4 cup/2 fl oz
  chopped capers

1 tablespoon each chopped
parsley and chives

2 teaspoons lemon juice

Tartar
Sauce

Method

1 Mix all ingredients in a bowl until blended. Leave to stand for 1 hour before serving. Serve tartar sauce with breaded calamari, or any other fish or seafood snack.

MAKES 1 1/2 CUPS/350 ML

Ingredients

1 x 210 g/7oz can pink salmon,
drained

250 g/8oz cream cheese

250 g/8oz finely diced celery

2 tablespoon lemon juice

2 teaspoons chilli

2 sheets lavash bread

Salmon
Pinwheels

Method

1 Mix salmon with cream cheese, celery, lemon juice
and chilli.

2 Spread half of the mixture evenly onto each sheet of
lavash bread. Roll up firmly, to make log shapes.
Slice and serve immediately.

MAKES 12–16

Ingredients

2 eggs, separated

50 g/2 oz butter, melted

500 g/1 lb powdered sugar

2 tablespoons cocoa

1 teaspoon vanilla

1 packet plain sweet biscuits, crushed

Biscuity
Chocolate Blocks

Method

1 To achieve an interesting texture, do not crush the biscuits for these quick and easy bites too finely; rather break them into 1 cm/1/2 in pieces.

2 Place egg yolks in a large mixing bowl and add the butter, sugar, cocoa and vanilla. Whip egg whites and add crushed biscuits. Add egg yolk mixture to egg white mixture and blend well. Press into a square greased baking tin. Refrigerate until set (at least 3 hours), and cut into squares with a very sharp knife.

MAKES 36

Ingredients

8 tablespoons butter

$^2/_3$ cup powdered sugar

$^1/_2$ cup/4 fl oz golden syrup

2 teaspoons grated rind of lemon

1 cup/9 oz flour

1 teaspoon ground ginger

2 teaspoons brandy

1 cup/9 fl oz thick
  whipping cream

$^1/_4$ cup/$1^1/_2$ oz powdered sugar

2 teaspoons rum

pinch salt

Brandy
Snaps

Method

1 Preheat the oven to 350 °F. Place butter in a saucepan. Add sugar and syrup and melt over a low heat. Stir until smooth. Remove from heat. Allow to cool slightly and add brandy and lemon rind. Sift flour, salt and ginger into the butter mixture and stir until well blended. Leave to cool for 3 minutes.

2 Drop teaspoonfuls of mixture onto a greased baking tray, leaving ample space in between for the brandy snaps to spread.
Bake for 8 minutes. Remove biscuits from the oven. Roll each biscuit loosely around the buttered handle of a wooden spoon, working quickly before the biscuits

set. Leave on the handle until biscuits have set in rolled up shape. Leave them to cool on a wire rack. If biscuits harden before shaped, return to the oven for a few minutes until they are pliable.

3 Whip cream, powdered sugar and rum until thick. Pipe into brandy snap tube from both ends. Serve immediately since cream will make the brandy snaps soggy. Baked and shaped brandy snaps will keep well in an airtight container for a few days.

50 MINUTES, MAKES 30, MODERATE

Feeling extravagant and ready for a challenge?

Prepare these brandy snaps with care, pat yourself on the back and enjoy

the compliments. They are delicious with or without a filling.

Ingredients

20 prawns

1 cup/250 g corn flour

1 teaspoon paprika

2 teaspoons grated lemon rind

1 tablespoon chopped parsley

1 egg, beaten

vegetable oil for deep-frying

sliced lemon to serve

Butterflied
Prawns

Method

1 Peel and de-vein prawns, leaving tails intact. Cut along
the back of each prawn and spread open (butterfly)
1 hour before frying. Refrigerate until required.

2 Combine corn flour, paprika, lemon rind and parsley.
Dip prawns into beaten egg and coat with corn flour
mixture. Heat oil in a heavy-bottomed saucepan.
Deep-fry prawns for 1–2 minutes in hot oil until
opaque. Drain on kitchen paper. Serve immediately
with sliced lemon.

MAKES 20

Prawns cook in minutes, and are usually easy to find,

although they are expensive. These prawns can also be cooked

under the grill or stir-fried.

Ingredients

60 g/2¹/₂ oz butter

1 teaspoon salt

2 cups/500 g self-rising flour

1¹/₃ cups milk

1 egg, beaten

1 teaspoon crushed garlic

150 g/5 oz grated cheddar

grated parmesan or sunflower seeds or
    sesame and caraway seeds

Cheese
Bread

Method

1 Preheat the oven to 425 °F. Rub butter into flour and salt. Add milk, beaten egg, garlic and cheddar cheese and mix well until dough is smooth.

2 Place in a well-greased bread pan. Sprinkle with parmesan cheese or sunflower seeds. Bake for 45 minutes. Reduce heat to 400 °F and bake for another 10 minutes. Slice and serve warm with savory butter.

MAKES 1 LOAF

Cheese bread is always a favorite.

Try this easy recipe and enjoy the compliments.

Cheese
Platter

Method

1 Make up a selection that includes both soft and hard cheeses. Serve with biscuits and fresh fruit and ensure that you have enough cheese knives. The following cheeses are readily available and good to use:

- HARD Double Gloucester, Gruyère, Pecorino, Cheddar

- SEMI-HARD Marbier, Raclette, Emmenthal, Feta

- SOFT Brie, Camembert, Danon

- BLUE-VEINED Gorgonzola, Roquefort, Stilton

- FRESH Mascarpone, Ricotta

Ingredients

250 g/9 oz butter

200 g/7 oz dark chocolate

2 tablespoons strong coffee

3 eggs

350 g/12 oz powdered sugar

1 cup/250 g flour

1 teaspoon baking powder

1 teaspoon vanilla

200 g/7 oz walnuts, chopped

salt

CHOCOLATE FUDGE TOPPING

40 g/1 1/2 oz butter

100 g/ 4 oz dark chocolate

40 g butter

300 g/10 oz powdered sugar, sifted

salt

1 teaspoon vanilla essence

1/2 oz/3 fl oz milk

chopped nuts

Chocolate
Brownies

Method

1 Preheat the oven to 375 °F. Place butter and chocolate, broken into pieces, in a double boiler and melt. Allow to cool slightly and add coffee. Beat eggs and sugar until light and fluffy. Gradually add coffee chocolate mixture. Sift flour, baking powder and salt and fold into chocolate mixture. Add vanilla and nuts.

2 Spoon mixture into a greased baking tin and bake for 30–40 minutes until firm to the touch in the center. Allow to cool in baking tin.

MAKES 40

3 To make chocolate fudge topping, melt butter and chocolate in a double boiler. Add icing sugar and salt and stir. Add milk and beat mixture until smooth. Remove from heat and place the saucepan into a bowl of ice water to cool down. Beat constantly until mixture thickens. Spread over chocolate brownie cake and sprinkle with chopped nuts. Allow to set and cut into squares.

Rich, chewy brownies packed with nuts are best topped with

chocolate fudge or chocolate icing. Use pecan nuts instead

of walnuts, or equal quantities of walnuts and pecans.

Ingredients

1 x 185 g/6 oz can tuna, drained

500 g/1 lb sweet potato or
potato, cooked and mashed

1 tablespoon yellow curry paste

1 tablespoon coriander

1 tablespoon plain flour

250 g/ 8 oz shredded coconut

oil for frying

Curried
Tuna Bites

Method

1 Place tuna, sweet potato, curry paste, coriander, flour and coconut into a bowl and mix well. Shape into small balls.

2 Fry in a little hot oil until golden brown. Drain on kitchen towels and serve hot. To keep warm, place in a single layer on baking sheets lined with kitchen towels and place into the oven at 315ºF for up to 30 minutes.

MAKES 25–30

Ingredients

500 g/1 lb smoked mackerel

3/4 cup butter

juice of 1/2 lemon

freshly ground black pepper

pinch paprika

2 tablespoons cream

choice salad greens, washed
    and crisp

Mackerel
Paté

Method

1 Skin and remove bones from mackerel and flake flesh. There should be approximately 375g/12 oz of fish or more. Beat butter until soft and creamy, add mackerel flesh and beat well. Add lemon juice and season with freshly ground pepper and a small pinch paprika. Beat in cream until just combined. Spoon into a small earthenware pot, cover and chill.

2 Serve with Melba toast, hot toast or crisp crackers.

MELBA TOAST

1 Lightly toast thinly sliced bread. As soon as it is ready, remove crusts, halve diagonally and slice each piece through horizontally. Place on a baking tray and bake in a slow oven 300ºF until crisp and pale golden. Cool. If preparing in advance, store in an airtight container.

SERVES 4

Serve with hot toast, Melba toast or crisp crackers.

Ingredients

500 g/1 lb calamari

2 eggs, beaten

1/2 cup/110 g flour, seasoned

500 g/1 lb breadcrumbs

vegetable oil for deep-frying

lemon slices dipped in chopped dill

toothpicks for dipping

Breaded
Calamari

Method

1 Rinse calamari, pat dry and remove spine and skin if necessary. Cut into 1 cm/1/2 in rings. Place flour in a bag and toss the calamari rings to coat. Dip each ring into the egg, allow excess to drip off and coat with breadcrumbs.

2 Heat oil in a heavy-based saucepan. Deep-fry several calamari rings at a time until golden brown. Drain on kitchen paper. Serve warm with lemon slices and Tartar sauce (see page 78). Provide toothpicks for dipping.

MAKES 40

Calamari is traditionally served with Tartar sauce or serve with sweet and sour chilli sauce as an alternative. The calamari can be prepared ahead of time. Refrigerate and fry just before serving.

Ingredients

1 English cucumber, halved
  lengthwise

2 teaspoons lemon juice

1 teaspoon salt

3 tablespoons chopped chives

125 g/4^1/$_2$ oz smooth cottage cheese

200 g/7 oz smoked salmon, cut into strips

18 toothpicks

2 tablespoons chopped dill

Cucumber
Salmon Delights

Method

1 Cut cucumber into ^{1}/$_2$ in/1^1/$_2$ cm chunks, place on a
flat plate and sprinkle with lemon juice, salt and
chives. Spread cottage cheese over salmon strips.
Dab cucumber chunks on kitchen paper to remove
excess lemon juice.

MAKES 18

2 Wrap each cucumber chunk in a strip of salmon and
secure with a toothpick. Garnish with a dollop of
cottage cheese and sprinkle with more chopped chives.
Refrigerate until required.

Cucumber, salmon and cottage cheese make a great combination.

This is a light and healthy snack.

Ingredients

1 cup sugar

2 cups/1 pint vinegar

2 teaspoons curry

1/2 cup/50 g corn flour

1 pineapple, sliced
    and quartered

110 g/4 oz golden raisins

toothpicks to serve

Curried
Pineapple

Method

1 Place sugar, vinegar and curry in a saucepan and bring to the boil over a low heat. Add corn flour to thicken the curry sauce, then add pineapple and raisins. Simmer until pineapple and raisins are soft, but pineapple must be firm. Remove from heat and allow to cool.

2 Refrigerate pineapples in curry sauce until required.

MAKES 36

Make this in advance and keep in the refrigerator.

Add some zing to a platter of cold meats or sausages.

Ingredients

400 g/12 oz puff pastry

1 egg, beaten

smooth apricot jam

1 cup/8 fl oz thick cream

50 g/2 oz powdered sugar

1 teaspoon vanilla

24 mint leaves to serve

Easy
Jam Tarts

Method

1 Preheat the oven to 415°F. Roll out puff pastry to ¼ in/5 mm thickness and cut into 1½ in/4 cm rounds. Cut out center 1 in/2.5 cm of half the rounds. Brush full rounds with egg, place a holed round on each full round, brush with egg and arrange rounds on a greased baking tray. Bake for 15 minutes until puffed out and golden brown.
Allow to cool.

MAKES 24

2 Spoon 1 teaspoon of jam into each pastry case. Whip cream, powdered sugar and vanilla. Top each jam tart with a dollop of cream and a mint leaf.

Buy ready-made vol-au-vent pastry cases and you can have these

ready in a few minutes. Use strawberry jam for variation.

Ingredients

100 g/4 oz feta cheese, cubed

40 g/1^1/$_2$ oz pesto

8 cherry tomatoes

fresh basil leaves

16 toothpicks

Feta
and Tomato Kebabs

Method

1 Feta cheese can be replaced with mozzarella or any other semi-hard cheese that takes your fancy. (For something really special, use whole, boiled quail eggs instead of cheese. For medium-hard eggs, place quail eggs in a saucepan, cover with water, bring to a boil and boil for 1^1/$_2$ minutes. Remove from the saucepan and rinse with cold water. Peel eggs and coat with pesto.)

2 Coat feta cubes with pesto and refrigerate overnight. Halve tomatoes. Thread tomato halves, basil leaves and feta cheese onto toothpicks. Serve with more pesto on the side.

MAKES 16

Ingredients

kiwi fruit, peeled and cubed

1/2 pineapple, diced

3 wedges lemon, cubed

bunch of grapes

1 red apple, cubed

lemon juice

10 skewers

passion fruit pulp

1/2 cup/4 fl oz thick cream

2 tablespoons powdered sugar

2 teaspoons medium–cream sherry
    (optional)

Fruit
Sosatie

Method

1 Toss cubed fruit in lemon juice to prevent discoloring. Thread fruit onto skewers, varying colors, shapes and flavors. Drizzle passion fruit pulp over.

2 Whip cream, powdered sugar and sherry. Serve sosaties with whipped cream on the side.

MAKES 10

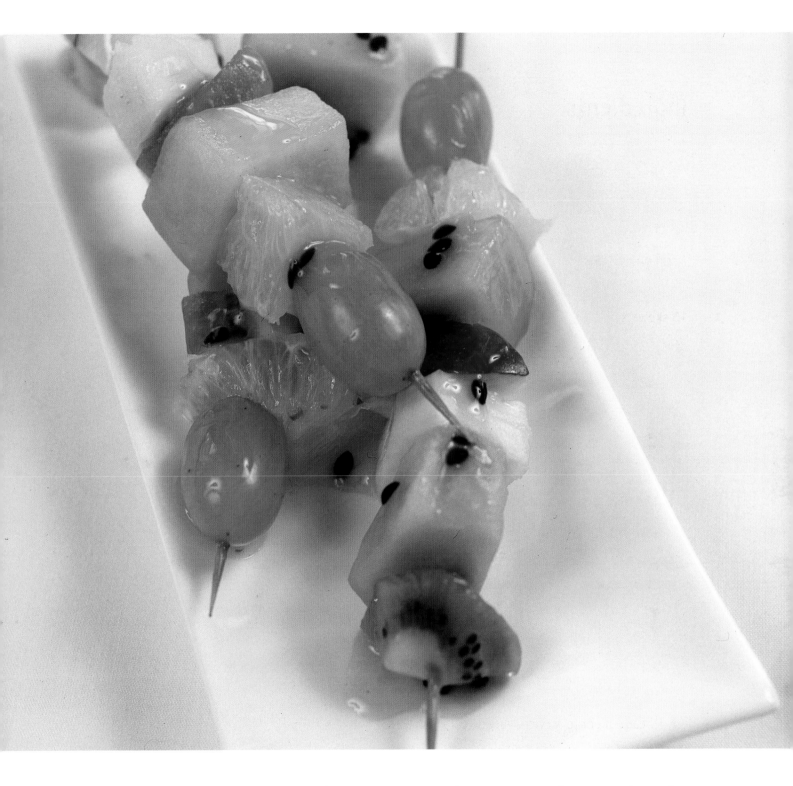

Make the best use of fruit in season and put together a pleasing

combination of colors, textures and flavors. Leave the skin on red apples

to add color, but wash them thoroughly before cutting them into cubes.

Use fresh mint leaves to add a special touch.

Gâteau
of Crêpes

Ingredients

1 cup/250 g flour

pinch salt

2 eggs, beaten

1 cup/8 fl oz milk

25 g/1 oz butter, melted

500 g/1 lb smooth cottage cheese

1 heaped tablespoon honey

1 heaped tablespoon lemon juice

1 tablespoon chopped dill

1 tablespoon chopped chives

300 g/10 oz smoked salmon, thinly sliced

Method

1 To make the crêpes, place flour and salt in a mixing bowl. Combine eggs and milk. Make a well in the center of flour. Add milk mixture to flour little by little, gradually working flour into milk. Beat with a wooden spoon or electric beater until smooth and free of lumps. Add melted butter, mix well and leave for 1 hour. Cook crêpes in a crêpe pan or flat skillet.

2 Mix cottage cheese, honey, lemon juice, chopped dill and chives. Place a crêpe on a cutting board. Cover with a thin layer of filling, followed by sliced salmon. Add another crêpe, cover with filling, followed by sliced salmon. Repeat until you've used 5 crêpes, top with a crêpe. Make another gâteau. Refrigerate overnight for filling to set. Cut away rounded edges so that you are left with a square. Cut into rectangles and serve on lettuce on top of round canapés or Melba toast. Alternatively, use a biscuit cutter and make rounds before starting the filling process.

MAKES 2, 12 SLICES EACH

Making the crêpes is a little time-consuming,

but the results are delicious. If you are in a hurry, buy

10 ready-made crêpes.

Ingredients

24 ready made individual

  meringue nests

CREAM FRUIT PUREE

1 cup/8 fl oz cream

1^1/$_2$ tablespoons powdered sugar

1 teaspoon vanilla

^{1}/$_2$ cup/4 fl oz puréed

  kiwi fruit, gooseberries or

  blueberries

COFFEE CREAM

2 eggs

2 tablespoons powdered sugar

2 tablespoons strong coffee

1 cup/8 fl oz thick

  cream

2 tablespoons coffee liqueur

Meringue
Nests with Fillings

Method

1 Treat family and friends to these mouth-watering treats that will only take a few minutes to prepare. Fill with one or more of the following fillings: Creamed Fruit Purée, Coffee cream, or Custard and Fruit.

2 To prepare Creamed Fruit Purée Filling, beat cream, powdered sugar and vanilla until thick. Add puréed fruit, and spoon into meringues. Decorate with fresh fruit used for purée.

MAKES 24

3 To prepare Coffee Cream, beat eggs and powdered sugar until light and fluffy. Add strong coffee and thick cream and beat until peaks form. Stir in coffee liqueur and refridgerate for 1 hour. Spoon into meringues and decorate with grated chocolate.

4 Fill meringue nests with thick custard. Top with an interesting variety of fresh berries, grapes, chopped fruit or passion fruit pulp and a dollop of thick, fresh cream.

Ingredients

250 g/8 oz firm white fish fillets,
   cubed

1 small green pepper, diced

1 small red pepper, diced

pineapple pieces (optional)

12 cherry tomatoes

toothpicks

MARINADE

3/4 cup butter, melted

2 tablespoons chopped dill

2 teaspoons crushed garlic

1 1/2 tablespoons chopped parsley

2 teaspoons lemon juice

Mini
Fish Kebabs

Method

1 The kebabs can be prepared the day before and refrigerated, covered in their marinade, but bake them just before serving.

2 Thread cubes of fish alternated with red and green pepper and pineapple (if using) onto toothpicks. End off with fish.

3 Place kebabs on a baking tray. Combine ingredients for the marinade. Pour the marinade over kebabs and stand for 1 hour, turning at least once. Preheat the oven to 350 °F. Bake kebabs for 10 minutes. Remove from the marinade. Serve warm, garnished with a cherry tomato at the end of each toothpick.

MAKES 12

Ingredients

1¹/₂ cups flour

2 teaspoons instant yeast

2 teaspoons salt

2 tablespoons olive or sunflower oil

1¹/₄ cups/10 fl oz warm water

TOPPING

110 g/4 oz tomato and onion mixture

2 teaspoons herbs (oregano, marjoram, rosemary)

1 teaspoon crushed garlic

250 g/8 oz grated mozzarella

Mini
Pizzas

Method

1 Mix the dough by hand or in a food processor. Place flour in a bowl and add yeast and salt. Combine oil and water. Make a well in dry ingredients and add water. Mix to combine, forming a sticky dough. Cover and leave in a warm place for 1 hour to rise until double the original size. Knock down and roll out 5-10 mm thick on a floured surface. Cut into rounds with a scone cutter and arrange on a greased baking sheet.

MAKES 24

2 Preheat oven to 425°F. Spread pizza bases with tomato and onion mixture. (Use the tinned, ready-made variety or fry chopped onion, tomatoes and garlic in olive oil.) Sprinkle with herbs and garlic and top with a generous amount of grated mozzarella. Bake for 8-10 minutes until golden brown and crisp around the rim of the base.

If time is a factor, buy ready-made pizza crusts and add your own topping.

This basic topping can be enhanced with just about anything that strikes

our fancy: chopped mushrooms and pineapple; black olives, grated Pecorino

and feta; artichokes and green olives; red and green peppers,

eggplant and baby carrots.

Ingredients

4 slices bread

1½ cups/12 fl oz milk

1 small onion, chopped

2 tins (170 g/6 oz each) tuna

3 eggs, beaten

1 teaspoon dried mustard

250 g/8 oz grated Cheddar

2 tablespoons mayonnaise

salt and freshly ground

  black pepper

Mini
Tuna Frittatas

Method

1 Preheat oven to 350 °F. Remove crusts from bread and soak in milk in a large bowl. Add rest of ingredients and mix well. Spoon into greased muffin pans. Fill pans almost to the top as the frittatas do not rise. Bake for 15 minutes or until golden and set.

2 These frittatas are delicious served warm or at room temperature. They keep well, so you can make them the day before and refrigerate in an airtight container. Remove from the refrigerator 2 hours before serving.

MAKES 12

Ingredients

1 cup/8 fl oz milk

2 eggs, beaten

2 cups/500 g flour

2 teaspoons baking powder

1 teaspoon salt

vegetable oil for deep-frying

Mini
Vetkoek

Method

1 Beat milk and eggs. Sift together dry ingredients to combine. Add milk mixture little by little to dry ingredients and mix to a thick, sticky batter.

2 Heat oil in a deep, heavy-based saucepan. Drop tablespoonfuls of the mixture in oil and fry until golden brown and puffed up. Drain on kitchen paper. Fill with savory mince or serve with butter, jam and cheese.

MAKES 24

These traditional deep-fried puffs can be dressed up or down with

a variety of fillings or butter and spreads. Served warm and filled

with savory mince, they are ideal for a light lunch.

Use teaspoonfuls of batter for a smaller version.

Ingredients

4 small or 1 large pita bread

1 cup/9 oz tomato sugo,
   tomato pulp or your favorite
   tomato pasta sauce

4 slices pastrami or smoked beef or

6 slices of beef salami, cut into strips

1 red or green pepper, cut into strips

2 tablespoons shredded gruyère or
   cheddar cheese

1/2 cup/100 g grated parmesan
   cheese, optional

Pita
Pizzas

Method

1 Toast pita bread under preheated grill. Heat tomato sugo or sauce and spread over each pita. Scatter meat and pepper over pita, top with cheese. Bake pizzas in preheated hot oven 400°F for 10-15 minutes or until golden and crisp around the edges, or grill under preheated grill, positioning not too close to the grill to prevent burning. The large pizza is cut into four.

SERVES 4

Ingredients

1 kg/2 lb mussels

pesto with basil

cherry tomatoes, halved

CHEESE TOPPING

butter for sautéing

1 onion, finely chopped

2 tomatoes, finely chopped

salt and pepper

1¹/₂ tablespoons crushed garlic

200 g/7 oz grated Cheddar

Mussels
in Half-Shells

Method

1 Prepare mussels as described on page 38. Top half mussels with pesto and halved cherry tomatoes.

2 Make the cheese topping for the remainder of mussels. Heat butter in a saucepan, add onion, tomatoes, and then salt, pepper and garlic. Cook until onion is tender. Spoon the mixture into mussel shells. Sprinkle with grated cheese. Grill for about 5 minutes or until cheese has melted.

MAKES 24

For an interesting combination of flavors and colors,

use both a pesto topping and a cheese topping. Serve with

freshly sliced, buttered French loaf.

Ingredients

125 g/4½ oz ricotta cheese

1 tablespoon each chopped parsley
   and basil or chives

1 tablespoon chopped spring onions

2 teaspoons lemon juice

freshly ground pepper

6–8 slices smoked beef or pastrami

8–12 small bamboo skewers

6 green spring onions,
   cut into short lengths

24 red or yellow cherry tomatoes

selection of salad greens

Skewered
Beef Rollettes

Method

1 Combine ricotta cheese, herbs, onions and lemon juice. Season to taste. Spread cheese mixture on slices of beef and roll up firmly. Pack into container, cover and chill until required.

2 Cut each roll into two or three. Thread beef rollettes on skewers alternating with lengths of onion and cherry tomatoes. Serve on salad greens with light mayonnaise, if desired, on the side.

SERVES 6

These rollettes may be served with a rice or pasta salad, or arrange

small quantities on cocktail sticks and serve with drinks.

Ingredients

5 wedges melon

15 slices parma ham

toothpicks

freshly ground black pepper

Parma Ham
and Melon

Method

1 Cut melon into bite-size chunks. Wrap each chunk in Parma ham and secure with a toothpick. Sprinkle with black pepper.

2 Alternatively, use thinly sliced smoked beef or smoked salmon instead of parma ham. Ring the changes with other firm tropical fruit in season such as papino, pineapple and mango.

MAKES 15

Use any variety of melon for this snack, or more than one to add color,

and you'll have it all wrapped up.

Ingredients

500 g/1 lb filo pastry

2 cups/16 fl oz milk

1/4 cup/50 g sugar

3 tablespoons custard powder

2 tablespoons corn flour

1 cinnamon stick

2 tablespoons butter

pinch of salt

1 teaspoon vanilla essence

4 tablespoons melted butter

cinnamon sugar for
    sprinkling

Filo
Custard Rolls

Method

1 Take filo from the freezer the day before you want to use it and defrost in the refridgerator. Unroll on a dry kitchen towel, cover with a dry kitchen towel and place a damp kitchen towel on top. Keep filo covered like this while you're not using it, since it dries out quickly when exposed to air.

2 Mix 2 tablespoons milk, sugar, custard powder and corn flour to a paste. Place remaining milk in a saucepan with cinnamon and butter and bring to the boil over low heat. Remove cinnamon stick. Add custard paste to milk mixture, stirring constantly until the mixture thickens. Remove from heat and add salt and

vanilla. Cover with wax paper or cling wrap to prevent skin from forming and set aside to cool.

3 Preheat the oven to 400 °F. Cut filo into 2 x 4 in/5 x 10 cm rectangles. Place a teaspoonful of filling in the center 1 in/3 cm away from one short end. Roll up pastry to cover filling. Lightly holding the filling in place, fold in the 2 sides and roll up all the way.
Place on a greased baking sheet with the open end down, brush with melted butter and bake for 20 minutes until golden brown. Remove from the oven and sprinkle with cinnamon sugar.

MAKES 24

Sausage Platter

Method

1 Most supermarkets and delis nowadays sell a wide range of processed sausages. This certainly makes for easy entertaining. Make a selection of these sausages, heat them up and cut into bite-sized lengths. Serve tempting dips and sauces on the side. The following sausages are readily available:

• Bratwurst (mainly pork or pork and veal). Grill to cook.

• Bockwurst (veal and pork). They are parboiled, so heat in boiling water.

• Cheese grillers (pork with cheese). Grill to cook frankfurters and viennas (beef and pork finely minced). Heat in boiling water.

• Russians (spicy, coarsely textured pork). Grill to cook.

• Knackwurst (similar to frankfurters with strong garlic flavor). Heat in boiling water.

• Chipolatas (spicy cocktail sausage). Heat in boiling water.

• Cocktail pork sausages. Grill to cook.

Ingredients

1 cup flour	FILLING
2 teaspoons baking powder	1 onion, chopped
pinch of salt	1 tablespoon butter
pinch of cayenne pepper	1 tomato, peeled and chopped
4 tablespoons butter	250 g/8 oz grated Cheddar
or margarine	1 egg, beaten
250 g/8 oz grated Cheddar	salt and freshly ground
1/2 cup/41/2 fl oz milk	black pepper
	sprigs of dill to garnish

Savory Cheese Puffs

Method

1 Preheat the oven to 350 °F. Sift dry ingredients to combine. Rub in butter. Add cheese, then milk and mix to a firm consistency. Do not over-mix. Bake in small, well-greased patty pans for 10 minutes.

2 Make filling. Sauté onion in butter. Add chopped tomato. Add cheese and egg and cook over a low heat until egg is done.

MAKES 24

3 Slice off top of each cheese puff. Spoon filling onto bottom half and replace top, shaped like wings. Garnish with sprigs of dill.

These bites are baked in small patty pans. Although just a mouthful,

their filling makes them well worth the effort.

Ingredients

250 g/8 oz fish fillets

250 g/8 oz cooked, shelled mussels

500 g/1 lb shrimp

1 red pepper, diced

2 large baby carrots, diced

8 wooden skewers

honey and curry sauce

Seafood
Kebabs

Method

1 Adding shrimp to these kebabs makes them rather rich. Marinate the kebabs in honey and curry sauce (see below).

2 Cut fish into cubes and peel shrimp, leaving tails intact. Thread mussels, fish and prawns alternated with red peppers and baby carrots on skewers.

MAKES 16

Place in a shallow oven proof dish and cover with honey and curry sauce. Allow to stand for 1 hour. Grill in sauce, turning frequently, until fish is tender and shrimp are opaque. If served cold, the kebabs can be grilled well in advance. Store in the refrigerator.

Honey
and curry sauce

Ingredients

10 tablespoons/5 oz butter

1/2 cup/4 1/2 fl oz honey

4 teaspoons curry powder

2 teaspoons chopped dill

2 teaspoons crushed garlic

Method

1 Melt the butter in a saucepan. Add the rest of the ingredients and stir continuously to blend.

MAKES 250 ML

Ingredients

¹/₄ cup/50 g ground almonds

1¹/₂ tablespoons butter, soft

2 teaspoons honey

2 teaspoons sherry

6 fresh apricots, halved and stoned

Bulgarian yogurt

Stuffed
Apricots

Method

1 Mix almonds, butter, honey and sherry together. Spoon into apricot hollows. Place under a heated grill for 1 minute. Don't overcook as apricot's skin will pop.

2 Top with a dollop of Bulgarian yogurt before serving.

MAKES 12

Ingredients

50 g/2 oz ricotta

2 teaspoons chopped almonds

8 slices streaky bacon, halved

16 plump pitted prunes

toothpicks

Stuffed
Prunes in Bacon

Method

1 Mix ricotta and almonds and pipe into prunes.
Wrap each prune in a bacon strip and secure with a
toothpick. Grill for about 4 minutes, turning frequently,
until bacon is crisp. Serve warm.

MAKES 16

or a vegetarian alternative, omit the bacon and serve the stuffed prunes cold.

You can use smooth cottage cheese instead of ricotta.

Ingredients

185g/6 oz smoked salmon

3 tablespoons crème fraîche or
   sour cream

1 tablespoon soft unsalted butter

good pinch of greated lemon rind

4 spring onions, white part only,
   chopped

1 tablespoon fresh lemon juice

1 tablespoon snipped dill

freshly ground black pepper

Rillettes
of Smoked Salmon

Method

1 Reserve $1/3$ of smoked salmon slices. Process the rest in a food processor with crème fraîche, butter and lemon rind. Transfer to a bowl and mix in remaining ingredients, including reserved smoked salmon, diced finely, adding a little pepper to taste.

2 Use two wet spoons to form mixture into oval mounds, arranging 2 or 3 mounds on each plate. Garnish with a little dill and salad greens if you wish and serve with toast.

SERVES 4

Ingredients

1¹/₂ cups/350 g flour

2 teaspoons baking powder

pinch of salt

2 eggs, beaten

1 cup/8 fl oz milk

1 tin (420 g/16 oz) sweetcorn

vegetable oil for frying

Sweetcorn
Fritters

Method

1 Sift together flour, baking powder and salt. Combine eggs and milk, add to dry ingredients and mix to a smooth batter. Add sweetcorn.

2 You can sprinkle these fritters with cinnamon sugar to serve as a sweet snack. Alternatively, add 110 g/4 oz bacon to the batter and top with grated cheese to serve as a savory snack. Heat oil in a frying pan.

Drop tablespoonfuls of batter in oil and fry until golden-brown on the underside. Turn and fry on the other. Drain on kitchen paper. Add desired topping and serve warm.

MAKES 24

Keep these fritters small so that they are easy to handle as finger food.

Ingredients

600 g/1¹/₄ lb dark chocolate

90 g/3¹/₂ oz unsalted butter

1 cup/9 fl oz thick cream

3 tablespoons brandy or rum

500 g/1 lb icing sugar, sifted

90 g/3¹/₂ oz cocoa, sifted

Truffles

Method

1 Melt chocolate and butter in a double boiler or in the microwave oven, stirring occasionally. Remove from heat, add cream, brandy and icing sugar and mix until smooth. Cover with wax paper or cling wrap and cool in the refrigerator until firm enough to handle. Shape into small balls and toss in cocoa.

MAKES 40 SMALL

Easy to make, these rich, irresistible sweets are good anywhere, any time.

They keep well in the freezer, so make a good quantity and set some aside.

Ingredients

2 kg/4 lb pork spareribs,
    trimmed of excess fat

2 onions, chopped

2 tablespoons fresh
    parsley, chopped

1 cup/8 fl oz chicken stock

2 tablespoons lemon juice

8 tablespoons/4 oz butter, melted

4 small fresh red chillies,
    chopped

HONEY-SOY MARINADE

4 cloves garlic, chopped

2 spring onions, chopped

1 tablespoon fresh ginger,
    finely grated

1 1/2 cups/12 fl oz
    rice-wine vinegar

1/2 cup/4 fl oz
    reduced-salt soy sauce

1/2 cup honey

Honey-Glazed Spareribs

Method

1 To make marinade, combine chillies, garlic, spring
    onions, ginger, vinegar, soy sauce and honey in
a non-reactive dish. Add ribs, toss to coat, cover and
marinate in the refrigerator for at least 4 hours.

2 Drain ribs and reserve marinade. Cook ribs, basting
    occasionally with reserved marinade, on a
preheated hot barbecue grill for 8–10 minutes or until
ribs are tender and golden. Place on a serving platter,
cover and keep warm.

SERVES 8

3 Place remaining marinade in a saucepan, add onions,
    parsley, stock and lemon juice and bring to a boil.
Reduce heat and simmer for 15 minutes or until the sauce
reduces by half. Pour mixture into a food processor or
blender and process to make a purée. With motor running,
pour in hot melted butter and process to combine.
Serve the sauce with spareribs.

Ingredients

1 lemon

750 g baby new potatoes,
   halved if large

2 cloves garlic, sliced

2 tablespoons olive oil

salt and black pepper

1 tablespoon butter

50 g/2 oz pitted green
   olives, quartered

Baby New Potatoes
with Lemon and Olives

Method

1 Preheat the oven to 425°F.
Halve lemon. Squeeze the juice from 1 half and chop the other half into small pieces.

SERVES 4

2 Toss potatoes, lemon juice, chopped lemon, garlic and oil together. Season, then arrange in a single layer in a shallow roasting tin and dot with butter. Cook for 25–30 minutes, shaking the tin occasionally, until potatoes are tender and golden brown. Stir in olives just before serving.

These tasty little potatoes are roasted with some of the best-loved

flavors of the Mediterranean: garlic, lemon and olives.

Ingredients

375g/12 oz pack ready-rolled
   puff pastry

1 tablespoon olive oil

200 g/7 oz red onions, halved and
   finely sliced lengthways

1 small red chilli, seeded and
   thinly sliced

salt and black pepper

2 tablespoons red pesto

25 g/1 oz pine nut kernels

Red Onion
and Chilli Tarts

Method

1 Preheat the oven to 425°F. Open out pastry sheet and cut out 1½ x 1½ in/4 x 4 cm rounds. Use a slightly smaller cutter or a sharp knife to score a ½ in/1 cm) border on each – this will form the rim. Place the rounds on a baking sheet.

2 Heat oil in a large frying pan. Fry onions for 10 minutes or until softened, stirring. Add chilli and cook gently for 1 minute, then season.

3 Spread pesto over the pastry rounds, leaving the rim clear. Spoon the onion mixture over pesto and scatter over pine nut kernels. Cook for 12–15 minutes, until the pastry has risen and is golden brown.

SERVES 4

These little tarts are packed with spicy flavor and are best

eaten fresh from the oven. If you want to, serve them with

some cooling Greek yogurt on top.

Ingredients

6 pitted green olives,
   finely chopped

1 tablespoon chopped
   fresh tarragon

1 tablespoon chopped fresh chives

1 tablespoon chopped fresh mint

2 teaspoons finely grated lemon rind

250 g/8oz tub ricotta cheese

black pepper

4 tablespoons sun dried
   tomato purée

1 large 5-cereal baguette, cut
   into 1/2 in/1 cm thick slices

1 clove garlic, halved

Ricotta Herb Dip
with Garlic Toasts

Method

1 Mix together olives, tarragon, chives, mint and lemon rind, then stir in ricotta. Season with pepper and mix well.

2 Lightly stir sun dried tomato purée into the ricotta mixture to create a marbled effect, then spoon into a serving dish.

SERVES 4

3 Preheat the grill to high. Grill baguette slices for 1–2 minutes on each side, until golden. Rub the cut surfaces of garlic halves over the toast slices and serve with the dip.

This unusual light summery dip is really easy to make and full of flavor.

The nutty-textured baguette slices, with a hint of garlic,

are perfect for dipping.

Ingredients

1 kg/2 lb lamb leg steaks,
    cut into 2½ cm/1 in pieces

250 g/9 oz ready-to-eat
    dried apricots

2 tablespoon finely chopped
    fresh mint

salt and black pepper

2 lemon, cut into 16 wedges

MARINADE

1 clove garlic, crushed

2 tablespoons low-fat
    natural yogurt

1 tablespoon olive oil

1 teaspoon ground cumin

1 teaspoon ground coriander

1 teaspoon paprika

pinch of cayenne pepper

juice of 1 lemon

Spiced Lamb
and Apricot Kebabs

Method

1 To make the marinade, place garlic, yogurt, oil, cumin, coriander, paprika, cayenne and lemon juice in a large non-metallic bowl and mix well. Add lamb, turning to coat. Cover and place in the refridgerator for 1 hour to marinate. If using wooden skewers, place them in water to soak for 10 minutes.

SERVES 8

2 Stir apricots and mint into lamb and season. Thread the meat and apricots onto 8 metal or wooden skewers, placing a lemon wedge at both ends. Discard the marinade.

3 Preheat the grill to high. Place the kebabs on a baking sheet under the grill and cook for 8–10 minutes, turning occasionally, until the meat has browned. Spoon over the juices and serve.

Tender chunks of lamb are mixed with apricots and mint then
glazed with Moroccan spices.

Ingredients

grated rind and juice of 1 lime

25 g/1 oz powdered sugar

1 kg/2 lb watermelon

1 tablespoon finely shredded mint

toothpicks for serving

Watermelon
with Lime Syrup

Method

1 Place lime juice in a small saucepan with powdered sugar. Stir over a low heat to dissolve sugar, then boil for 1 minute or until reduced to a syrupy consistency. Pour into a jug and cool for 20 minutes, then refrigerate for 1 hour or overnight.

2 Cut the skin from watermelon, then remove and discard the seeds. Cut the flesh into bite-sized chunks, catching any juices in a bowl. Sprinkle watermelon chunks with mint and toss them together lightly.

3 Add reserved melon juice to the chilled syrup and pour over melon just before serving. Sprinkle with grated lime rind and serve with toothpicks.

SERVES 4

This is a deliciously refreshing combination of juicy chunks of

watermelon and a cold lime and mint syrup.

Ingredients

1 tablespoon dijon mustard

4 tablespoons red wine vinegar

1 teaspoon sugar

$1/2$ teaspoon salt

$1/2$ teaspoon ground black pepper

finely chopped parsley and snipped
   fresh chives to taste

$1/2$ cup/4 fl oz olive oil

1 bunch asparagus

Asparagus
with Vinaigrette

Method

1 For the vinaigrette, measure mustard into a bowl.
Whisk in vinegar, sugar, salt, pepper and herbs to taste.
Continue whisking, slowly adding oil until the mixture
thickens. Cover until ready to use.

2 Wash and trim asparagus and steam for 5–10
minutes until tender but crisp. Arrange on a plate
and drizzle with the vinaigrette. Serve warm or cold.

SERVES 2–4

Ingredients

$^1/_3$ cup/$2^1/_2$ fl oz olive oil

rind of 1 lemon

2 tablespoons lemon juice

60 g/$2^1/_2$ oz shallots, finely sliced

2 teaspoons oregano, chopped

freshly ground pepper and salt

750 g/$1^1/_2$ lb baby octopus, cleaned

salad leaves, for serving

Baby Octopus Marinated
in Olive Oil and Oregano

Method

1 In a bowl, mix together olive oil, lemon rind, lemon juice, shallots, oregano, and pepper and salt.
Add octopus, and leave to marinate for 1 hour.

2 Heat a chargrill pan, lightly brush with oil, add octopus, and cook (basting with the marinade) for 2–3 minutes, or until tender.

3 Serve on a bed of salad leaves.

SERVES 2–4

Ingredients

310 g/10$\frac{1}{2}$ oz ricotta cheese

310 g/10$\frac{1}{2}$ oz feta cheese

4 eggs

white pepper

1 packet filo pastry

$\frac{1}{2}$ cup melted butter

Cheese Triangles

Method

1 Pre-heat the oven to 400°F. Combine ricotta, feta and eggs in a bowl and mix well. Season with white pepper.

2 Brush 1 layer of filo pastry with melted butter, and place another layer on top. Cut the pastry, lengthwise, into 4 strips.

3 To shape the triangles, place a heaped teaspoon of cheese mixture close to the bottom of the right hand corner of the strip. Fold this corner over the mixture, diagonally across to the left-hand edge to form a triangle. Continue folding from right to left in a triangular shape to the end of strip. Brush the top of each triangle with melted butter and place on a baking tray. Repeat until all mixture has been used.

4 Bake triangles in the oven for about 20 minutes (until they are golden). Note: To make larger triangles, cut the strips of pastry wider, and use more filling per triangle.

MAKES APPROXIMATELY 25 TRIANGLES

Ingredients

250 g/8 oz onion, minced

410 g/13 oz short grain rice

150 mL/5 fl oz oil

1 tablespoon dill, chopped

1/2 cup mint, chopped

1 tablespoon salt

40 small grape leaves

150 mL/5 fl oz lemon juice

Stuffed
Grape Leaves

Method

1 Mix onion, rice, oil, herbs, salt and lemon juice in a bowl. Boil some water and soak grape leaves in boiling water for 15 minutes. Then place under cold water for 10 minutes, and lie out on a kitchen towel to dry.

MAKES APPROXIMATELY 35-40

2 To wrap grape leaves, place 1 tablespoon of the rice mixture in the center of leaf and wrap like a parcel. (Use less mixture if the leaves are small.)

3 Place the leaves in a saucepan and cover with boiling water. Add 1/4 cup/2 fl oz of lemon juice to the water. Place a plate over the top of them and cook for 1 hour or until the grape leaves are cooked.

These stuffed grape leaves are also known as dolmades.

Impress your friends by making these tasty treats.

Ingredients

500 g/1 lb white bait (smallest variety
you can find)

60 g/2½ oz shallots, finely sliced

2 teaspoons dill, chopped

rind of 2 lemons

2 teaspoons lemon juice

½ cup/110 g flour

2 eggs, lightly beaten

freshly ground pepper and salt,
   to taste

olive oil, for frying

lemon wedges

White Bait
Fritters

Method

1 Place white-bait in a food processor and process
until well combined.

2 Transfer the mixture to a bowl and add shallots, dill,
lemon rind, lemon juice, flour, eggs, and pepper and
salt, and mix together.

MAKES 20 FRITTERS

3 Heat oil in a pan and add the mixture (1 tablespoon
per fritter) and cook for 2–3 minutes or until golden.
Serve with wedges of lemon.

Ingredients

500 g/1 lb asparagus

8 thin slices pancetta,
   cut into pieces

pecorino shavings

DRESSING

½ cup/3½ fl oz extra
   virgin olive oil

juice of 1 lemon

sea salt

freshly ground,
   black pepper

Asparagus with
Pecorino and Pancetta

Method

1 Trim off thick asparagus ends and cook asparagus in boiling water for 4 minutes, until tender but still crisp. Run under cold water, until asparagus is cool, then dry with kitchen paper.

SERVES 4–6

2 For the dressing, place lemon in a bowl, then slowly add oil, whisking, until the dressing is thick. Season with salt and pepper.

3 Pour the dressing over asparagus, and serve with pancetta and pecorino cheese shavings.

Ingredients

450 g/14 oz beef fillet, sliced into
   4 mm/¼ in slices

125 g/4½ oz arugula, washed

1 tablespoon balsamic vinegar

3 tablespoons extra virgin olive oil

pecorino cheese shavings

freshly ground black pepper

salt

Beef Carpaccio

Method

1 Lightly oil a sheet of greaseproof paper and season it lightly with salt and freshly ground black pepper.

2 Arrange 4 slices of beef on this (approximately 2 in apart). Place another oiled piece of greaseproof paper on top, and gently beat the meat, until it has spread out to at least twice its former size. Repeat with remaining meat slices.

SERVES 6

Refrigerate the meat until needed. Alternatively, partly freeze the meat, before slicing thinly.

4 Place some arugula in the center of a plate, arrange beef slices around arugula, and drizzle with balsamic vinegar and olive oil. Serve with shavings of pecorino cheese and black pepper and salt.

Ingredients

1 ciabatta loaf, sliced
in 2 cm/³/₄ in slices

¹/₄ cup/2 fl oz olive oil

60 g/2¹/₂ oz sun-dried tomato paste

180 g/6 oz bocconcini, each ball
sliced into 5 slices

110 g/4 oz basil leaves, sliced,
or whole leaves

Bruschetta with
Bocconcini and Basil

Method

1 Grill ciabatta slices on each side for 2–3 minutes.

2 Brush with olive oil, spread with sun dried tomato
paste, top with bocconcini slices and sliced basil
leaves, or whole leaves, if preferred. Serve immediately.

SERVES 6

This simple but delicious treat will satisfy your guests.

Ingredients

1 kg/2 lb calamari, cut into
   thin rings

1/2 cup/3 fl oz lemon juice

3 cloves garlic, crushed

1/2 cup/4 1/2 fl oz olive oil

DRESSING

1/4 cup/2 1/2 fl oz lemon juice

1/2 cup/3 1/2 fl oz olive oil

1 1/2 tablespoons parsley,
   chopped

1 garlic clove, crushed

1 teaspoon dijon mustard

salt and pepper

Marinated Calamari
with a Lemon
and Herb Dressing

Method

1 Place lemon juice, garlic and olive oil in a bowl, add calamari, and marinate for at least 3 hours. If time permits, marinate overnight.

2 For the dressing place all ingredients in a bowl or jar and whisk well or until the dressing thickens slightly.

SERVES 4–6

3 Heat 1 extra tablespoon of oil in a pan, add calamari, and cook for a few minutes, until it is cooked through. Alternatively, calamari can be cooked on a chargrill plate.

4 Serve calamari with the dressing drizzled over.

Ingredients

2 quantities of pizza dough (see
   page 116)

50 mL/¼ cup chilli oil

4 potatoes, thinly sliced

2 small red onions, thinly sliced

3 sprigs rosemary, chopped

arugula

Potato and Onion
Pizza with Chilli Oil

Method

1 Preheat the oven to 475°F.

2 Dust a baking tray with flour. Dust bench with flour, take one piece of dough and press out with your hands to form a thick disc.

3 Roll-out dough in one direction, turn 90 degrees, and roll again in one direction, repeating this process until dough forms an 3 in/8 cm circle.

MAKES 8 PIZZAS

4 Place on a baking tray and brush with the chilli oil, top with potato, onion and rosemary, and bake for 5–10 minutes, or until brown. Top with arugula before serving, and drizzle with a little oil.

Note: Variations of toppings can be used: arugula and parmesan; sun-dried tomatoes, bocconcini and basil.

Ingredients

¹/₄ cup/2 fl oz extra
   virgin olive oil

3 tablespoons lemon juice

2 teaspoons small whole capers

350 g/11 oz smoked salmon, allow
   3–4 slices per person

1 tablespoon parsley,
   roughly chopped

1 small red onion,
   finely chopped

freshly ground black pepper

extra capers to garnish

Smoked Salmon
with Extra Virgin
Olive Oil and Lemon

Method

1 Combine oil, lemon juice, and capers in a bowl, and whisk.

SERVES 4

2 Arrange smoked salmon and onion on serving plates.

3 Drizzle the dressing over smoked salmon, sprinkle with parsley and freshly ground black pepper, and serve. Garnish with extra capers.

Ingredients

30 medium mussels

2 shallots, finely chopped

1 sprig thyme

2 sprigs parsley

1 bay leaf

$^1/_2$ teaspoon salt

$^1/_2$ cup/4 fl oz white wine

$^1/_2$ cup 4 oz butter or
margarine, softened

1 tablespoon parsley,
chopped

2 cloves garlic, crushed

1 tablespoon chives

Baked
Mussels

Method

1 Scrape the beard and wash mussels thoroughly.
Place in a large saucepan with shallots, thyme,
parsley and bay leaf.

2 Sprinkle over salt and then add wine. Steam for 5
minutes or until the shells have opened. Open
mussels and discard the lids.

SERVES 4

3 Divide mussels in the remaining half shells into 4
ovenproof dishes. Make a herb butter by combining
butter, parsley, garlic and chives and place a generous
portion on each mussel.

4 Bake at 370°F for approximately 3 minutes or until
butter has melted.

Ingredients

500 g/1 lb crab meat, flaked

4 tablespoons butter, softened

1 tablespoon dijon mustard

$^1/_8$ teaspoon Tabasco® sauce

2 egg yolks

110 g/4 oz fresh breadcrumbs

salt

flour

oil for deep-frying

TARTAR SAUCE

250 g/8 oz egg mayonnaise

1 teaspoon finely chopped onion

1 teaspoon finely chopped parsley

1 teaspoon finely chopped basil

1 teaspoon finely chopped gherkins

1 teaspoon finely chopped
    green olives

1 teaspoon dijon mustard

salt and pepper

Deep-Fried Crab Balls

Method

1 To make sauce, combine all ingredients in a bowl and refrigerate until ready to use.

2 Combine crab meat, butter, mustard, Tabasco sauce, egg yolks and breadcrumbs in a bowl. Mix well, and add salt to taste. Cover and refrigerate until firm.

MAKES ABOUT 36

3 Shape into balls the size of a small walnut and return to refrigerator for 30 minutes. Roll balls in flour and deep-fry in hot oil until golden. Drain on kitchen towels. Serve with the Tartar sauce (see page 78).

Ingredients

1/3 cup/3 1/2 fl oz virgin
   olive oil

1 onion, finely chopped

1 red pepper, diced

4 vine-ripened tomatoes, diced

1/2 stick celery, sliced

2 cloves garlic

1 kg/2 lb clams, cleaned
   and sand removed

2/3 cup/5 fl oz dry white wine

1 tablespoon freshly chopped
   aromatic herbs (thyme,
   rosemary, marjoram)

salt and pepper

Clam Provençal

Method

1 Place oil, onion, pepper, tomatoes, celery and garlic
   in a large cooking pot. Cook over high heat for 5
minutes, stirring frequently to prevent sticking.

SERVES 4–6

2 Add clams, white wine, fresh herbs and seasoning,
   and cook with the lid on until all the shells have
opened. Stir frequently to ensure even cooking.

3 When clams are open, serve in large bowls with
   salad or grilled baguette.

Complement these lovely clams with a rosé or white wine from Provence.

Ingredients

12 small pink potatoes
(such as Pontiacs)

12 small white potatoes

salt and pepper to taste

1 tablespoon olive oil

150 g/5 oz smoked salmon,
finely chopped

3 tablespoons sour cream

2 tablespoons red onion,
finely chopped

2 teaspoons prepared white
horseradish

$^1/_2$ bunch of chives, finely chopped

50 g/2 oz smoked salmon, thinly
sliced, cut into 48 squares
cut into 24 squares)

drained capers to garnish

salmon caviar to garnish

extra chives to garnish

Baby Potatoes Filled
with Smoked Salmon

Method

1 Preheat the oven to 400°F. Cut all potatoes in half and mix with oil in a large bowl. Season to taste with salt and pepper, then place potato halves cut-side down on an oiled baking sheet. Bake potatoes until just tender (about 20 minutes), then cool completely.

2 Meanwhile, mix together finely chopped smoked salmon, sour cream, red onion, horseradish and chives in a small bowl and season with salt and pepper.

3 When you are ready to assemble potatoes, use a melon baller or a small spoon to scoop out some of

potato from the cut-side, then cut a thin slice off the rounded end of each potato so that each potato-half will stand upright. Spoon 1 teaspoon of salmon filling into each potato cavity, then place on a tray ready to serve.

4 Garnish each potato with a small slice of smoked salmon, some salmon caviar and chives. Chill for up to 2 hours before serving.

MAKES 48

These elegant but very easy appetizers will start your party off with a bang!

Remember to use Atlantic or Tasmanian smoked salmon because

these are not too highly smoked.

Champagne makes a superb accompaniment.

Ingredients

115 g/4 oz prepared squid,
  cut into rings

2 tablespoons seasoned flour

1 egg

2 tablespoons milk

olive oil, for frying

sea salt

lemon wedges, to serve

Fried Squid

Method

1 Toss squid rings in seasoned flour in a bowl. Whisk egg and milk together in a separate bowl. Heat oil in a heavy-based frying pan.

2 Tip out the floured squid rings, one at a time, into the egg mixture, shaking off any excess liquid.

SERVES 4

Place into hot oil, in batches if necessary, and fry for 2–3 minutes on each side until golden.

3 Drain fried squid on kitchen paper, then sprinkle with salt. Move to a small warm plate and serve with lemon wedges.

Ingredients

1 kg/2 lb mussels, cooked
  mariniéres style (see page 226)

GARLIC BUTTER

2¼ cups softened butter

2 cloves garlic, minced

1 tablespoon chopped fresh parsley

2 tablespoons brandy

salt and pepper

arugula to serve

Escargot
Mussels

Method

1 Remove the extra half-shell and keep mussel in 1 shell.

2 To make the garlic butter, combine all ingredients in a bowl and mix well.

SERVES 4

3 Top up the half–shell mussel with garlic butter. Grill mussels until sizzling and serve topped with arugula.

Ingredients

500g/1 lb chicken mince

10 shallots, finely chopped

1/4 teaspoon five spice powder

1 1/2 tablespoons honey

1 teaspoon lemon zest

2 tablespoons lemon juice

350 g/12 oz fresh breadcrumbs

oil for frying

toothpicks

PLUM SAUCE

1 cup oz plum jam

1/2 cup/4 oz white vinegar

1/4 teaspoon ground ginger

1/4 teaspoon ground allspice

1/8 teaspoon hot chilli powder

Cocktail Chicken
with Plum Sauce

Method

1 In a food processor, place all ingredients, except frying oil, and process together quickly. With wetted hands, shape into small balls. Place on a flat tray in a single layer and refrigerate for 30 minutes.

2 Heat oil, at least 2 in/5 cm deep in a frying pan, or half full in a deep fryer, to 350°F. Deep-fry for about 3-4 minutes. Remove and drain on kitchen paper. Place a toothpick in each ball and arrange on a platter. Place the plum sauce in a bowl and serve with the chicken balls.

3 To make the plum sauce, place all ingredients in a small saucepan and bring slowly to a boil while stirring. Simmer for 2 minutes. Remove from the heat and cool. Pour into a small bowl.

SERVES 4

Ingredients

milk to glaze

SOUR CREAM PASTRY

300 g/2½ cups plain flour

pinch of salt

180 g/6 oz butter

1 egg

⅓ cup/3 fl oz sour cream

FILLING

1½ tablespoons butter or oil

1 onion, finely chopped

500 g/1 lb chicken mince

250 g/8 oz canned peach slices,
   chopped finely

salt and pepper to taste

Chicken Empanadas

Method

1 Sift flour and salt into a bowl, add butter and rub in with your fingertips until fine like breadcrumbs. Mix egg and sour cream together, add to the flour mixture and mix to a dough. Wrap in cling film and refrigerate for 30 minutes.

2 To make the fillings, heat butter in a frying pan, add onions and sauté a few minutes. Add chicken mince and stir while cooking until mince changes color to white and then to a slightly golden color. Stir in chopped peach, and salt and pepper to taste. Allow to cool.

MAKES 15–25

3 Roll out dough between 2 sheets of wax paper. Remove the top sheet. Cut rounds of pastry about 4–4½ in/10–12 cm diameter. Place a heaped teaspoon of the filling in the center of each round, moisten the edges with water and fold over. Pinch the edges well together or press with the prongs of a fork. Glaze with a liitle milk and bake in a preheated oven at 400°F for 10–15 minutes. Serve hot or cold as finger food, a snack, or a meal with vegetable accompaniments.

Ingredients

2 eggs, lightly beaten

salt and pepper

2 cups/250 g breadcrumbs

1 tablespoon dry mixed
    aromatic herbs

1 kg/2¼ lb clams cleaned, cooked
    mariniéres style and removed

from shell (see page 226)

3 tablespoons Tartar sauce

arugula to serve

Fried Vongole

Method

1 Place eggs in a bowl and season with a little salt and
pepper. Combine breadcrumbs and herbs in a
separate bowl.

2 Dip clams in the egg mixture, then roll in
breadcrumbs.

SERVES 4

3 Deep-fry clams in hot oil, until golden brown.
Drain on kitchen paper and serve immediately with
tartar sauce (see page 78) and arugula.

Ingredients

1 kg/2 lb chicken wings

2 tablespoons oil

4 tablespoons grated
   fresh ginger root

2 cloves garlic, crushed

1 tablespoon soy sauce

2 tablespoons sugar

3 tablespoons sherry

50 g/2 oz toasted sesame seeds

Ginger Wings

Method

1 Fold back the wing tip to form a triangle. Place wings in a large baking dish. Mix remaining ingredients together, except the sesame seeds, and pour over wings.

2 Place in a preheated oven at 350°F and cook for 25–30 minutes until brown and cooked through. Turn once during cooking. Remove from the oven and arrange on a platter. Sprinkle over sesame seeds and serve.

SERVES 8-10

Ingredients

20–24 large oysters in the half- shell

coarse sea salt

2 tablespoons/1 oz butter

1 small leek, washed and finely sliced

salt and freshly ground pepper

pinch of sugar

squeeze of lemon juice

$^1/_2$ cup/$4^1/_2$ fl oz dry white wine

pinch of saffron threads
or curry powder

$^1/_2$ cup/$4^1/_2$ fl oz cup
cream

1 egg yolk

salt and white pepper to taste

lemon wedges to serve

Hot Oysters
and Leeks

Method

1 Remove oysters from their shells, wash and keep chilled.

2 Melt butter in a frying pan and toss leek in hot butter. Season with salt, freshly ground pepper and sugar, cover tightly and cook gently until tender. Season with lemon juice.

3 Boil wine with saffron or curry powder over a moderate heat until reduced by half. In a small bowl, combine cream with egg yolk and whisk. Whisk in the hot wine mixture and return to a gentle heat, if necessary, to thicken slightly, whisking all the time. Do not let it boil. Add salt and white pepper to taste and remove from the heat.

4 Arrange cooked leeks in the oyster shells, and place oysters on top. Coat each oyster with the sauce and place under a preheated hot griller for a minute or so to glaze. Serve immediately with lemon wedges.

SERVES 4

Ingredients

1kg/2 lb chicken breast fillets	BATTER
oil for deep–frying	2 egg whites
slices of lemon to serve	¼ cup/50 g flour
MARINADE	¼ cup/2 fl oz lemon juice
2 tablespoons soy sauce	DIPPING SAUCE
¼ cup/2 fl oz sherry	reserved marinade
2 teaspoons grated fresh ginger	½ cup/4½ oz chicken stock
2 teaspoons lemon zest	2 tablespoons lemon juice
2 teaspoons sugar	2 tablespoons corn flour

Lemon Chicken Fingers

Method

1 Cut breast fillets into ½ in/1 cm wide strips from the long side of fillet. Place strips in a non-metal dish. Combine marinade ingredients, pour over strips, mix well and allow to marinate for 30 minutes.

1 To make the batter, stiffly beat egg whites to the soft peak stage, fold in flour and lemon juice. Remove strips from the marinade, reserving the marinade.

SERVES 4

2 Heat oil in a deep–fryer to 350°F. Dip a few strips at a time into the batter and deep–fry them for 5 minutes until golden. Drain on kitchen paper. Repeat with the remainder.

3 To make the dipping sauce, pour reserved marinade into a saucepan, add chicken stock and bring to a boil. Mix to a smooth paste lemon juice and corn flour, stir into the saucepan, lower the heat and stir until the sauce boils and thickens. Serve as finger food with the dipping sauce and slices of lemon, or as an entrée with the sauce and a salad garnish.

Ingredients

12 raw king prawns, peeled

2 tablespoons olive oil

2 tablespoons sherry

few drops Tabasco® sauce

salt and freshly ground black pepper

lemon wedges to serve

King Prawns
in Sherry

Method

1 Make a superficial cut down the back of each prawn, then pull out and discard the dark intestinal tract.

2 Heat oil in a frying pan and stir-fry prawns for 2–3 minutes until pink. Add sherry and season with Tabasco sauce, salt and pepper. Tip into a dish and serve immediately with lemon wedges.

SERVES 4

Ingredients

8 medium red onions, unpeeled

8 rosemary sprigs

6 cloves garlic peeled and slivered

¼ cup/2 fl oz olive oil

2 tablespoons balsamic vinegar

1 tablespoon brown sugar

2 tablespoons red wine vinegar

¾ cup/16 fl oz vegetable stock

salt and freshly ground pepper to taste

Cipolle
Balsamico

Method

1 Preheat the oven to 375°F.Using a sharp knife, cut a thin slice off the base of each onion so onions will sit upright. Cut a thin slice from the top of each onion, and then cut small slits deep in the center. Insert 2 rosemary sprigs and 2 garlic slivers into each onion, then place onions in a small baking dish.

2 In a small bowl, stir together olive oil, balsamic vinegar, sugar, red wine vinegar and stock. Pour over onions, then place them in the oven and bake, basting a few times with the dish juices until onions are soft when pierced with the point of a sharp knife (1–1½ hours).

3 Before serving, split the skins of onions with a sharp knife and remove (or leave them as they are and let each diner do their own). Season onions to taste with salt and pepper.

SERVES 8

These wonderful onions must be baked unpeeled. The skins will help to

retain the full flavor of the onions and, after cooking, the skins will fall

away easily. The rosemary sprigs that are poked into the onions impart

a delicious flavor. These are wonderful as part of an antipasto platter.

Ingredients

50 button mushrooms

VINAIGRETTE

¹⁄₄ cup/2 fl oz red
 wine vinegar

salt and freshly ground pepper,
 to taste

³⁄₄ cup/6 fl oz olive oil

FILLING

2 x 170 g/6 oz cans crab meat,
 flaked

¹⁄₃ cup/3 fl oz mayonnaise

¹⁄₃ cup/3 fl oz finely chopped
 spring onion

¹⁄₃ cup/3 fl oz finely chopped
 parsley

1 cup/8 fl oz finely
 chopped walnuts

salt and freshly ground black pepper

Mushrooms Stuffed
with Crab and Walnuts

Method

1 Remove stems from mushrooms and discard. Wipe mushroom caps with a damp cloth. Brush inside with vinaigrette.

2 To make the vinaigrette, in a small bowl, combine vinegar, salt, and pepper. Whisk in oil and let stand 5 minutes. Whisk again, then taste and adjust seasoning.

MAKES 50

3 To make the filling, combine crab meat, mayonnaise, spring onion, parsley and walnuts. Mix well and season to taste with salt and freshly ground black pepper.

4 Place a heaped teaspoon of filling into each mushroom cap. Refrigerate until ready to serve.

Ingredients

2 kg/4½ lb mussels

½ cup/4½ fl oz dry
  white wine

2 tablespoons chopped onion

4 parsley stalks, bruised

6 black peppercorns, crushed

CRÊPES

½ cup/100 g plain flour

2 large eggs

mussel liquid (see Method)

4–6 tablespoons thickened cream

4 tablespoons butter

6 tablespoons fresh parsley,
  chopped

Mussel Crêpes

Method

1 Wash mussels, discarding any that are open (and do not close when touched). Pull off the beards. Place wine, onion, parsley stalks and peppercorns in a large sauce pan and bring to a simmer.

2 Add mussels (in 2 batches) and cover. Cook over a high heat for 3–4 minutes, shaking occasionally, until they are open. Discard the shells and any mussels that remain shut. Strain the liquid into a measuring jug and leave to cool. Taste for seasoning.

3 Make the crêpe batter. Place flour in a bowl or blender and work in eggs, mussel liquid and 2 tablespoons of cream. (Don't over-beat in a blender.) Allow to stand for 1 hour.

4 Melt 1 tablespoon of butter in a frying pan, swirling it around. Add to the batter and stir thoroughly.

5 To cook crêpes, heat another tablespoon of butter and swirl. Use about 175 mL/6 fl oz crêpe batter per crêpe. It is easiest to pour from a cup. Lift the pan and pour the batter fast into the middle of the pan and in a circle around, tilting the pan to cover the base. (If you overdo the liquid, spoon off anything that doesn't set at once. Crêpes should be thin.

6 Return the pan to the heat, shaking it to make sure the crêpe does not stick. Cook for 1 minute until golden underneath, then flip over using a spatula. Briefly cook the other side. Roll and keep warm on a plate while you make more.

7 Warm the remaining cream in a saucepan with the mussel bodies. Spoon mussels and a little cream onto 1 edge of a crêpe, sprinkle with parsley and roll up. Serve immediately.

SERVES 6

Ingredients

455 g/1 lb green or ripe olives

1 fresh oregano sprig

1 fresh thyme sprig

1 teaspoon finely chopped
  fresh rosemary

2 bay leaves

1 teaspoon fennel seeds, bruised

1 teaspoon finely crushed
  cumin seeds

1 fresh red chilli,
  seeded and chopped

4 cloves garlic, crushed

olive oil

Spiced Olives

Method

1 Using a small sharp knife, make a lengthwise slit
through to the pit of each olive. Put olives into a
bowl. Stir in oregano, thyme, rosemary, bay leaves,
fennel seeds, cumin seeds, chilli and garlic.

2 Pack the olive mixture into a jar with a tight–fitting
lid. Add enough oil to cover olives, seal and leave for
at least 3 days, shaking the jar occasionally, before using.

MAKES 6 SERVINGS

Ingredients

1 kg/2 lb potatoes, peeled

1 small onion, peeled (optional)

1 cup/9 fl oz olive oil

5 eggs, beaten

salt

Potato
Omelette

Method

1 Wash and dry potatoes, then cut into thin slices. If you are using onion, dice it finely.

2 Heat oil in a frying pan, add potatoes and onion, season and cover. Fry gently, moving the frying pan so that vegetables don't stick. Once potatoes are cooked (take care they don't become crisp, break them up a bit and remove from the pan with a slotted spoon. Add to beaten eggs. Stir potatoes around until they are well covered with egg. Add salt to taste.

SERVES 6–8 AS A TAPA

3 Remove most of oil from the frying pan, leaving about 1 tablespoon, and reheat. Have ready a plate with a slightly larger diameter than the pan. Return the egg and potato mixture to the pan and cook for a few minutes until one side is golden.

4 Next, and this is slightly tricky, slip the omelette out onto your plate, cooked side down, and then slip it back into the pan, cooked-side up. Cook until firm.

5 Your omelette should be about 1^1/$_2$ in/4 cm thick. If you are using it for tapas, then cut it into squares.

Ingredients

2 kg /4¹/₂ lb mussels

¹/₂ cup/3¹/₂ fl oz dry
  white wine

2 cloves garlic, crushed

4 slices Parma ham, finely chopped

85 g/3 oz fresh white breadcrumbs

2 tablespoons pesto

2 tablespoons grated
  fresh root ginger

Mussels in Ginger with
Pesto-Crumb Topping

Method

1 Scrub mussels. Soak them in cold water for 5 minutes, drain, then repeat. Remove any beards and discard any mussels that are open or damaged. Place in a large saucepan with wine and garlic. Cover and cook over a high heat for 3 minutes or until mussels open, shaking the sauce pan occasionally. Discard any mussels that do not open.

2 Remove mussels from the sauce pan and reserve the cooking liquid. Discard the top shell from each mussel and arrange mussels on the half-shell on a

baking sheet. Strain the mussel liquid through muslin or a clean kitchen towel. Combine ham, breadcrumbs, pesto and ginger and stir in 1–2 tablespoons of the mussel liquid to moisten.

3 Preheat the grill to high. Spoon a little crumb mixture onto each mussel, then cook under the grill for 2 minutes or until golden and bubbling.

SERVES 4

Ingredients

14 equal-sized mushroom caps
and stems

1 tablespoon butter, unsalted

4 spring onions

8 sun-dried tomatoes in oil, drained

1 tablespoon breadcrumbs, dried

salt and pepper to taste

3 tablespoons Parmigiano, grated

4 tablespoons pesto, either

bought or home-made

PESTO

500g/1 lb basil leaves, fresh and
tightly packed

2 cloves garlic, peeled

110 g/4 oz pistachio nuts, toasted

75 g/3 oz parmesan cheese, grated

$1/2$-1 cup/$4^1/_2$-9 fl oz olive oil

salt and pepper to taste

Pesto-Stuffed
Mushroom Caps

Method

1 Preheat the oven to 400°C. Remove mushroom stems and finely chop the stems with 2 mushroom caps. Sauté these in butter with spring onions until soft. Remove from heat and add chopped sun dried tomatoes, breadcrumbs and salt and pepper, to taste. Add half grated cheese and mix well.

2 Brush the inside of mushroom caps with pesto and carefully fill each cap with an even quantity of filling. Place on an ungreased baking tray and sprinkle with remaining cheese. Just before serving, bake mushrooms for 10 minutes or until hot and just firm enough to handle. Serve on a small plate with a fork if necessary.

3 To make basil pesto, place basil, garlic, nuts and cheese in a food processor and process until finely chopped. Add olive oil through the feed-tube while the motor is running. Stop adding oil when the pesto is of a consistency you like. Season to taste with salt and pepper to taste.

MAKES 14

These mushroom caps can be filled up to 8 hours ahead, and then

baked just before you are ready to serve them.

Ingredients

1 tablespoon butter

1 tablespoon olive oil

2 cloves garlic, minced

1 brown onion finely chopped

200 g/7 oz wild mushrooms (such as Swiss brown, porcini, shiitake)

1 tablespoon flour

2 tablespoons water or stock

50 g/2 oz chives finely chopped

50 g/2 oz basil finely chopped

6 sheets puff pastry

50 g/2 oz pistachio nuts, toasted and finely chopped

2 tablespoons cilantro, finely chopped

2 tablespoons chives, finely chopped

1 tablespoon parsley, fresh and finely chopped

$^1/_2$ cup/4 oz good quality store-bought mayonnaise

salt and pepper to taste

Wild Mushroom Palmiers
with Herb Mayo

Method

1 Preheat the oven to 425°F. Heat butter and oil in a large frying pan and sauté minced garlic and finely chopped onion. Meanwhile, finely chop mushrooms in a food processor. Add these to onion mixture and cook gently for 5 minutes. Sprinkle flour over the mushroom mixture, and stir to incorporate. Add water or stock and stir until the mixture thickens and boils. Allow to cool thoroughly before adding chopped chives and basil.

2 Lie a sheet of pastry on a flat surface. Spread one-sixth of the cooled mushroom mixture over pastry and sprinkle with one-sixth of the finely chopped nuts. Fold opposite sides of pastry in to meet in the middle, then fold again so that pastry looks like a compact "log." Lie the log on its side and gently press down firmly. Slice the mushroom-filled log into 8 slices and lie each on a greased oven tray. Repeat with remaining pastry and filling ingredients.

3 Freeze the uncooked pastry for 5 minutes, then bake for 12–15 minutes or until golden brown.

4 To make the herb mayonnaise, mix herbs and mayonnaise together and allow the flavors to blend for at least 30 minutes. Season with salt and pepper, and serve with the pastries.

MAKES 40 SMALL PASTRIES

These pastries freeze well, both cooked and uncooked, so you can

make these days or weeks ahead, and then defrost and bake them,

or refresh in the oven, before serving.

Ingredients

1 teaspoon vegetable oil

1 teaspoon sesame oil

3 cloves garlic, crushed

3 fresh red chillies, chopped

1 kg/2 lb uncooked medium
   prawns, shelled and deveined

1 tablespoon brown sugar

$^1/_3$ cup/3 fl oz tomato juice

1 tablespoon soy sauce

Stir-Fried
Chilli Prawns

Method

1 Heat vegetable and sesame oils together in a wok over a medium heat, add garlic and chillies and stir-fry for 1 minute. Add prawns and stir-fry for 2 minutes or until they change color.

2 Stir in sugar, tomato juice and soy sauce and stir-fry for 3 minutes or until the sauce is heated through.

SERVES 4

Ingredients

1 kg/2¹/₄ lb mussels, cleaned

1 small onion, sliced

1 stick celery, sliced

1 clove garlic, chopped

¹/₄ cup/2 fl oz water
   or white wine

pepper

1 tablespoon butter

1 tablespoon parsley, chopped

Mussels
Mariniéres

Method

1 Place mussels, onion, celery, garlic and water
  (or white wine) in a large saucepan.

2 Cook over a medium heat until mussels have
  opened. Stir frequently to ensure mussels
cook evenly.

3 Add pepper to taste. Stir in butter and parsley just
  before serving.

SERVES 3–4

Ingredients

250 g/8 oz short grain white rice

1 cup/8 fl oz water

¼ cup/2 fl oz rice or
   white vinegar

2 tablespoons sugar

½ teaspoon salt

10 sheets nori seaweed

½ cucumber, thinly sliced

¼ red pepper, cut in strips

1 ripe avocado, sliced

2 x 125 g cans smoked tuna slices,
drained

Simple Sushi

Method

1 Place rice into a sieve and rinse under cold water until the water runs clear. Drain and place into a saucepan with measured water. Stand for 30 minutes. Combine vinegar, sugar and salt and set aside to dissolve.

2 Place rice over a high heat, bring to a boil and boil for 1 minute. Cover the saucepan, lower the heat and simmer gently for 20 minutes. Stand for 10 minutes,

then transfer to a bowl. Stir the vinegar mixture into rice and continue stirring gently until rice is cool and vinegar is absorbed.

3 Cut each seaweed sheet into 2 rectangles. Place a spoonful of rice at one end, top with a slice of cucumber, a strip of red pepper and a slice each of avocado and tuna. Roll up to form a horn shape. Continue with remaining ingredients. Cover and refrigerate until needed.

MAKES 20

Ingredients

5 tablespoons/2$\frac{1}{2}$ oz margarine
  or butter

1 cup/9 fl oz water

1 teaspoon chili powder

1 cup/9 fl oz plain flour

3 eggs, lightly beaten

1 x 340 g/12 oz can asparagus
shoots and tips, drained

110 g/4 oz diced tasty cheese

50 g/2oz finely grated
  Parmesan cheese

oil for deep-frying

Asparagus
and Cheese Puffs

Method

1 Place margarine, water and chilli into a saucepan and bring to a boil. Remove from the heat, then immediately add flour and beat with a wooden spoon until smooth. Return to heat and beat until the mixture forms a ball. Remove form the heat and allow mixture to cool.

MAKES 40

2 Using an electric mixer or a food processor, beat eggs into cooled mixture until the mixture is soft, but still holds its shape. Stir in asparagus and cheeses. Drop teaspoonfuls of mixture into hot oil and fry until puffed and golden brown. Drain, and serve hot.

Ingredients

4 eggs, lightly beaten

¼ cup/2 fl oz milk

2 tablespoons plain flour

1 x 185 g/6 oz can tuna and onion,
drained

1 teaspoon chilli powder

2 zucchinis, grated

½ red pepper, finely diced

250 g/8 oz grated tasty cheese

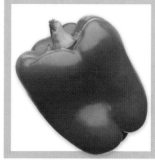

Tuna
Chilli Slices

Method

1 Place eggs, milk and flour into a bowl and whisk until smooth. Stir in tuna and onion, chilli, zucchinis, red pepper and cheese.

2 Pour into a greased and baking paper-lined 7½ in x 10 in/18 cm x 27 cm lamington tin and bake at 350ºF for 30–35 minutes, until set. Cut into fingers and serve warm or cool.

MAKES 24

Chilli
Smoked Oysters

Ingredients

2 x 85 g/3½ oz cans smoked oysters,
 drained

½ teaspoon chilli powder

2 tablespoons spring onions,
chopped

1 small ripe tomato, diced

2 teaspoons balsamic vinegar

crusty bread to serve

Method

1 Place oysters into a shallow glass or ceramic dish.

2 Place chilli, spring onions, tomato and vinegar into a bowl.
Stir to combine and pour over oysters. Cover and marinate in the
refrigerator for 20 minutes, then serve with lots of crusty bread.

MAKES 15-25

Moroccan
Mussels

Ingredients

2 x 85 g/3½ oz cans mussels,
 drained

1 teaspoon ginger, garlic and
shallots stir-fry mix

2 teaspoons coriander

1 teaspoon ground cumin

½ tablespoon extra virgin olive oil

2 tablespoons lemon juice

crusty bread to serve

Method

1 Place mussels into a shallow glass or ceramic dish.

2 Place stir-fry mix, coriander, cumin, olive oil and lemon juice into a
bowl. Whisk to combine and pour over mussels. Cover and marinate
in refrigerator for 20 minutes, then serve with lots of crusty bread.

SERVES 4

Ingredients

300g/10 oz chicken mince

2 tablespoons black bean
and garlic paste

2 tablespoons finely chopped
spring onions

2 tablespoons chopped
water chestnuts

1/4 cup/50 g breadcrumbs

20 spring roll wrappers

DIPPING SAUCE

2 teaspoons chilli sauce

2 tablespoons soy sauce

1 tablespoon honey

1 tablespoon lemon juice

Black Bean
Chicken Rolls

Method

1 Place mince, black bean paste, spring onions, water
chestnuts and breadcrumbs into a bowl and mix well.

2 Place spring roll wrappers onto a board and brush
edges with a little water. Place a tablespoon of
mixture onto each wrapper, fold sides in and roll up into
a cigar shape.

MAKES 20

3 Place rolls into an oiled steamer over boiling water
and steam for 10 minutes. Allow to cool slightly
before serving with dipping sauce.

4 For the dipping sauce, mix all ingredients. Serve in a
small dish.

Ingredients

1 chargrilled eggplant

handful marinated mushrooms

handful of semi-dried tomatoes

marinated artichokes

Mediterranean
Antipasto

Method

1 The ingredients are all available at the supermarket deli. Arrange on a party platter.

SERVES 4

Ingredients

1 cup/250 g self-rising flour

1 egg

3/4 cup/5 fl oz milk

1 tablespoon melted margarine
 or butter

2 tablespoons cilantro

1 tablespoon yellow curry paste

TOPPING

1 cup/9 fl oz sour cream

2 teaspoons red curry paste

250g/9 oz tuna slices, drained

cherry tomatoes and basil leaves
 to garnish

Cilantro Blinis with Tuna

Method

1 Blinis: Place flour into a mixing bowl and make a well in the center. Add egg, milk, margarine, cilantro and curry paste. Mix wet ingredients until smooth, stirring to gradually incorporate flour.
Mix until smooth.

2 Preheat a non-stick pan over a medium-low heat and brush with a little extra margarine. Drop spoonfuls of the mixture into the pan. When bubbles

MAKES APPROXIMATELY 48

appear on the surface, turn and cook the other side. Remove to paper towels to cool. Use at once or wrap, seal and freeze for up to 3 months.

3 For the topping, combine sour cream and curry paste. Spread a little of the mixture onto each blini, then top with a tuna slice,a wedge of cherry tomato and a basil leaf.

Ingredients

2 x 110 g/4 oz cans sardines, drained

1 teaspoon garlic

2 tablespoons extra virgin olive oil

1 tablespoon chopped parsley,
   finely chopped

finely grated rind and juice of lemon

crusty bread to serve

Marinated
Sardines

Method

1 Place sardines into a shallow glass or ceramic dish.

2 Place garlic, olive oil, parsley, lemon rind and juice
into a bowl. Whisk to combine and pour over
sardines. Marinate in the refrigerator for 20 minutes,
then serve with lots of crusty bread.

SERVES 4

Ingredients

250 g/8 oz cream cheese

2 tablespoons yellow curry paste

250 g/8 oz grated tasty cheese

50 g/2 oz golden raisins, chopped

50 g/2 oz poppy seeds

water crackers, celery sticks and
   fresh and dried fruit to serve

Poppy Seed Cheese Log

Method

1 Place cream cheese in a bowl, add curry paste and beat until smooth. Stir in grated cheese and raisins. Mix well.

2 Turn onto a sheet of aluminium foil, then mold into a log shape about 1 1/2 in/4 cm diameter. Wrap firmly and refrigerate for 1 hour or until firm. Unwrap and roll in poppy seeds.

3 Serve onto a platter with water crackers, celery sticks and fresh and dried fruits.

SERVES 8–10

Ingredients

2 tablespoons green curry paste

2 tablespoons coconut cream

2 sheets ready-rolled puff pastry

50 g/2 oz desiccated coconut

Spicy
Pastry Straws

Method

1 Mix curry paste and coconut cream. Spread half the mixture evenly over each pastry sheet. Sprinkle with coconut. Using a sharp knife, cut each pastry sheet into 1½ in/1 cm wide strips.

2 Holding each end, carefully lift each strip and twist. Place onto baking paper-lined baking slides and bake at 400°F for 10 minutes, until golden brown. Cool on racks and store in an airtight container for up to 2 weeks. Crisp in the oven just before serving.

MAKES 48

Ingredients

2 medium onions, sliced

110 g/4 oz roughly chopped
   cashews

2 teaspoons chilli

2 tablespoons ginger, garlic
   and shallots stir-fry mix

1 cup/250 g self-rising
   flour

1 egg, lightly beaten

¼ cup/2 fl oz soda water

oil for deep-frying

COCONUT CHUTNEY

2 tablespoons ginger, garlic and
   shallots stir-fry mix

1 teaspoon chilli

2 tablesppons desiccated coconut

½ cup/4 oz coconut cream

2 teaspoons lemon juice

Onion
and Cashew Fritters

Method

1 Place onions into a bowl. Add cashews, chilli and stir-fry mix, and mix well. Stir in flour. Add egg and soda water and mix well.

2 Heat oil in a saucepan over a medium heat. Add spoonfuls of the mixture and fry until golden brown and cooked through. This should take 5–6 minutes.

MAKES 24

Drain on kitchen towel and serve with coconut chutney. To keep warm, place in a single layer on baking slides lined with kitchen towel and place into a 315°F oven for up to 20 minutes.

3 To make Coconut Chutney, place all ingredients into a bowl and mix well.

Ingredients

1 tablespoon margarine or butter

1 small onion, finely chopped

1 tablespoon cajun spice mix

2 tablespoons finely chopped celery

2 tablespoons finely diced green pepper

1 x 185 g/6 oz can tuna, drained

2 teaspoons tomato sauce

250 g/8 oz cream cheese

burritos or flatbread to serve

Cajun Tuna Dip

Method

1 Melt margarine or butter over a medium heat. Add onion and cook until soft. Add spice mix and cook until very dark. Remove from the heat.

2 Add onion mixture, celery, green pepper, tuna, lemon juice and tomato sauce to cream cheese. Mix with a fork until mixture is combined. Cover and refrigerate until needed. Serve with burritos or flatbread, torn into pieces.

MAKES 15-25

Ingredients

2 tablespoons/1 oz unsalted butter,

softened

3 tablespoons brown sugar

2 tablespoons flour

1/2 teaspoon ground cinnamon

8 prepared pikelets or drop scones

strawberry conserve

440 g/14 oz canned peach halves,

drained

Peach
and Strawberry Pizza

Method

1 Place butter, sugar, flour and cinnamon in a bowl and mix to with a crumble consistency.

2 Heat pikelets or drop scones under a preheated medium grill for 1 minute or until just warm.

3 Turn pikelets or drop scones over, spread with conserve, then top with peach halves and sprinkle with butter mixture. Return to grill and cook for 5 minutes or until top is golden.

SERVES 4

These are sensational served with whipped cream or vanilla ice cream. Any combination of jam or conserve and fruit can be used. You might like to try blackcurrant jam with apples.

These are sensational served with whipped cream or vanilla ice cream.

Any combination of jam or conserve and fruit can be used.

You might like to try blackcurrant jam with apples.

Index

Index